THE SIERRA CLUB
SUMMER BOOK

WRITTEN AND ILLUSTRATED BY
LINDA ALLISON

SIERRA CLUB BOOKS / CHARLES SCRIBNER'S SONS

SAN FRANCISCO / NEW YORK

The Sierra Club Summer Book was developed and prepared for publication at The Yolla Bolly Press, Covelo, California under the supervision of James and Carolyn Robertson during the fall and winter of 1976-1977. Production staff: Sharon Miley, Loren Fisher, Gene Floyd, Jay Stewart, Michael Ludwig, and Evelyn Swift.

The Sierra Club, founded in 1892 by John Muir, has devoted itself to the study and protection of the nation's scenic and ecological resources — mountains, woodlands, wild shores and rivers. All Club publications are part of the nonprofit effort the Club carries on as a public trust. There are some 50 chapters coast to coast, in Canada, Hawaii and Alaska. Participation is invited in the Club's program to enjoy and preserve wilderness everywhere. Address: 530 Bush Street, San Francisco, California 94108.

LIBRARY OF CONGRESS CATALOGING IN PUBLICATION DATA

Allison, Linda.
THE SIERRA CLUB SUMMER BOOK

SUMMARY: A collection of animal facts and summer activities including craft projects and nature discussions.

1. Natural history — Juvenile literature. 2. Summer — Juvenile literature. 3. Handicraft — Juvenile literature. 4. Outdoor life — Juvenile literature. [1. Natural history. 2. Summer. 3. Handicraft. 4. Outdoor life] I. Sierra Club. II. Title.

QH 48.A44   796.5   76-57681
ISBN 0-684-15014-X
ISBN 0-684-15018-8pbk.

1 3 5 7 9 11 13 15 17 19 MD/C 20 18 16 14 12 10 8 6 4 2
1 3 5 7 9 11 13 15 17 19 MD/P 20 18 16 14 12 10 8 6 4 2

MANUFACTURED IN THE UNITED STATES OF AMERICA

CONTENTS

SUMMER IS THE TIME

Summer is the time of long light and short nights. Summer is lean back, kick off your shoes, school's out, and enjoy yourself time. Summer is probably the best time of the year.

Summer shows itself around the local swimming hole, in the fresh food department at the supermarket, in long lines at the ice cream store, in weedy cracks on the sidewalk, and around your sweaty collar.

Summer is bug bites on your ankles and showers twice a day. It's sticky sheets and fruit stains on your best shirt. It's the sound of lawn mowers and the smell of cut grass.

Summer is knowing your best friend leaves on vacation two days after you get back from yours. It's finding that all your crayons have melted together and that the birds have beat you to the berry bushes.

Summer is watermelon and the 4th of July. It's cricket noises and reruns on TV. It's your mother telling you to *please* go outside. Sometimes summer is secretly wishing you were back in school because you're bored out of your gourd. If you feel that there's nothing to do, this book is for you because it's all about summer.

It tells what's going on in the heavens to make it hot down here on earth. It has stories about animals and instructions for growing weird plants. There are directions for making collections of your natural finds. It has crafts projects like knob knitting and basic whittling with a pocketknife. There are hints on sleeping out and getting acquainted with nighttime critters and flitters; plus ways to keep cool, good stuff to send away for, games to play, and toys to make; not to mention some projects to get wet with at the beach, and things to think about while you're getting there.

This book is for anyone looking for a way to spend a summer day. So dig in. Summer is too good to waste.

SUMMER SEND AWAY

A lot of kids like to send away for things; they know how exciting ripping the cover off some long awaited item can be, and getting something in the mail can liven up an otherwise boring summer day.

This book has a lot of things you can send away for. Many of them are free, some of them cost money. They are sprinkled throughout this book wherever they seem to fit. Some are posters or charts that you can decorate your wall with and still learn a little something about natural history. Some are suggestions on where to get special equipment or information. Some are magazines that a beginning naturalist might want to look into. And some are freebies that are good sources of extra information in case you're interested.

A lot of free things are handed out by companies. Be prepared to get a commercial along with the information. Of course, like any advertising, take it with a grain of salt.

When you write away:

Tell them what you want exactly. Of course you can ask for any related information they might have, if you are interested.

Make sure that somebody else can read what you've written, especially *the return address* which should always be on your letter as well as on the envelope.

Be friendly. Don't feel you have to send off a formal adult-type request. Most people who open mail love letters from kids. Believe me, they get enough of the boring adult kind.

The cheapest letter you can write is on a postcard. You can help a non-profit organization like the ecology center to save money if you write a letter and enclose a stamped self-addressed envelope.

ACKNOWLEDGEMENT

The author thanks Ron Hennessey for sharing his insect wisdom, and Stella Allison Mann for contributing the garden section and other bits to this book.

1

CELEBRATION
OF LIGHT

SUMMER IS NOT THE SAME

Summer is the season of light. The time when the earth's tilt floods the sky with extra hours of longer, stronger light. However, those extra hours of light add up to different summers in different places.

Summer can be scorching dry, sauna-bath days where the heat presses right up against your skin and burns your toes on the sidewalk.

Summer can mean cool clouds of fog that hang over the land, sometimes burning away to sunshiny afternoons, sometimes not.

Summer in some places can be a sort of soggy endurance test. The air is humid, soup-like stuff that never lets you get cool. All summer long you stay sticky, hot, and excited about the onset of autumn. Ride your bike and you feel like you have been flogged with a hundred wet dish rags. This kind of summer leaves you dragging around and sticking close to the air conditioner.

In some places summer gets a late start, but makes up for it with a ferocious burst of plant and animal life. If you ever sample sum-mer in the far north like in Canada or Alaska, you'll notice that the sky is always light. Even at night, the sky is no darker than twilight. Plants grow wildly in the space of a few months. Birds fly in from the south to take advantage of the new food. The north is famous for its clouds of insects and swarms of mosquitos.

Summer slowly crawls up the mountains, reaching the high country last. The earth's highest places never thaw, remaining clothed in snow the year round.

Some places have great thundering rains in the summer, complete with electric-storm light shows. In other spots rain is a rarity. The only drizzle is from the dribble of lawn sprink-lers. There are some spots on earth where rain is a real event. In the Libyan Desert, it rains an average of only once every four years.

The wet places stay furry green the whole summer, not losing their color until the first frosts. The dry places take on a dusty, dull col-or during summer. Plants in these places rush through the spring, making their seeds. These seeds sit out the summer drought, waiting for the winter rains.

Even around your own backyard, summer varies on the sidewalk, under the lawn, and in the basement. You no doubt know where to go to find a little spring coolness when it feels like the Sahara out on the sidewalk.

Summer comes in many colors. It has many flavors. It's fun to watch it move over a place and make changes over the face of your local earth. If you do any traveling, don't forget to watch out for what summer is up to in other places.

Summer is not the same.

BRINGING IN SUMMER

The peoples of Europe had many ceremonies to greet summer. Many had to do with drowning or setting fire to winter or dancing around trees. It is thought that these customs are surviving bits of older religions in which fire and trees were worshipped.

In Silesian Villages — that's a region of Poland — a figure of death was dressed up and paraded around town. In the end it was torn to bits or thrown in a river with curses. In some places death was pelted with stones or set on fire. Whatever the method, death — the symbol of winter — was done in.

In death's place, a fir tree was carried back into town. The young people might have decorated it with paint, bits of colored cloth, paper roses, or egg shells. The tree was the spirit of vegetation, and it was called the "Summer" or "May."

Sometimes the spirit of summer took on a different form. The prettiest girl in the village would reign over the festivities. She would be called May Lady or Queen of the May. Sometimes it would be a man. In England he was known as the Greenman. Today in England the Greenman still survives. Many pubs use his name throughout the land. Come to think of it, he looks a lot like the Jolly Green Giant.

In some places the spirit of the May was a pole. This tree was stripped of its branches and decorated with ribbons. People danced around the pole. In some places they still do, although they would be surprised to know they were honoring the tree spirit.

BATTLE OF
SUMMER AND WINTER

In the past, towns in Sweden celebrated summer with a war. Two groups of young men met on horseback and clashed in mock battle. The leader of the winter group wore furs. The leader of summer was decked with flowers and leaves. Summer always won. After this fight there was feasting.

The Eskimos held a magical tug-of-war in the autumn; autumn is the visiting season before the dark cold winter. A group would divide, with "The Ducks" (summer-born people) on one side and "The Ptarmigans" (winter-born people) on the other side. A tug-of-war with a seal skin rope would commence. If "The Ducks" won, it meant that summer would triumph over winter, and the upcoming winter would be fair and mild.

SUN DANCE

The sun dance was the most important festival of the Plains Indian peoples, like the Kiowa and the Dakotas. The Dakotas called it gazing-at-the-sun-dance. It brought scattered bands of people together to renew friendships, to exchange news and property, and to arrange marriages. It was a happy time of spiritual unity among the people and the spirits of the earth.

The Plains people followed the buffalo, which scattered during the winter and then gathered in great herds to mate during the summer. The festival itself lasted for four days, although the Indians may have been gathering for a time before this. Ceremonies included offerings of smoke to the rising sun, asking for good weather, processions, gatherings, buffalo feasting, and dancing. A ceremonial pole was painted with special symbols and set in the ground.

On the fourth day, the buffalo dance was performed by warriors, four times. The warriors who received special help from the sun or earth spirits during the past year, performed the gazing-at-the-sun dance. To do this they would fix themselves to the pole and gaze at the sun and circle the pole on their toes to the sound of drums, songs, and the encouragement of the watching people. In some tribes the warriors would fasten themselves to the pole by sticking skewers under the muscles of their back or chest. They would dance until they pulled free. Visions often came to the person during or after the dance.

MIDSUMMER EVE: JUNE 24TH

Celebrating the longest day of the year is a tradition in North Africa. During the last century, fires in many parts of Europe blazed that day and into the night. In Sweden it was the most festive night of the year.

All sorts of magic was thought to be possible on Midsummer's Eve. People danced 'round the bonfires. Charred sticks were carried home to ward off spells and protect a house from lightning. Fire-jumping could foretell the height of the crops. In some places it could rid you of fleas. The fires were said to banish sickness, especially among cattle. A girl who saw nine bonfires was to marry within the year.

Celebration went on all night with debauchery until daybreak.

EQUINOX

Today our seasons proceed with clockwork regularity. Our understanding of the seasons is the result of thousands of years of eyeballing the sky by those with a talent for astronomy.

Most of us still secretly have the same seasonal sense as the ancient hunters and plowmen. To us summer starts on the first scorcher of the year, no matter what the calendar says.

Old earth peoples had some interesting ways of marking out summer. The Teutons had a summer which was followed up by winter and spring. Autumn didn't exist for them. In the tropics there are two seasons: wet and dry, neither being summer since the tropics get an equal amount of heat and light the whole year round. In some places seasons were thought of differently, such as the time-tne-fig-sprouts, or the time-the-migrating-crane-cries.

In some parts of the world people began to keep careful track of the sky. The Eskimos and the Arizona Indians noticed the turning points when the sun's position foretold the lengthening or shortening of the days. The Incas built towers at Cuzco to mark the sun's progress.

AN ANCIENT AND FAMOUS SUN TEMPLE

Stonehenge is a Stone Age monument in England built of huge, flat stones which sit in a circular pattern. The stones were dragged there in ancient times for a purpose we can only guess.

Not all of Stonehenge survives. Many of the giant stones were broken up to build bridges and such. It was a convenient quarry for later folks who didn't give a hoot for historical landmarks. Still there are enough stones standing for us to know it is a monument to the sun.

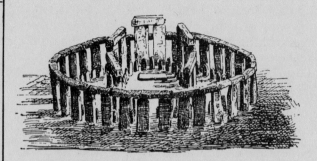

At the center of the curving side stones, there is an altar stone. Near this stone is another stone which casts a shadow on it on Midsummer's Day. The entrance was lined with a ceremonial avenue which faces the point on the horizon where the sun rose on the day of the solstice.

SUN, GIVER OF LIFE

As we use more energy, we are looking around frantically for new sources. It's only lately that we have really remembered that we are a one star planet. All our power comes from the sun. Without it earth life, as we know it, could not and would not be.

Many ancient folk seemed to know this. Maybe they didn't know about photons and photosynthesis, but they knew that without the sun, the snow wouldn't melt and the crops wouldn't grow. This they were sure of. Long ago the sun was honored as the giver of life.

The ancient Semites worshipped Shamash, the God of Light and Justice. The sun was one wheel on his chariot, which he rode daily across the sky. The Egyptians honored Ra as the supreme God and the Great Creator. Ra had many forms and names. The Inca's god of the sun was called Inti. Like the Egyptians, they believe their rulers to be descendents of the sun. The Aztecs worshipped a sun god called Tezcatlipoca, or Smoking Mirror.

SUN TAKER OF LIFE

The Incas made human sacrifices to the sun. These were on a small scale to the number of lives offered to the blood-thirsty Aztec sun, Tezcatlipoca.

The Aztecs believed they were created from the bones of an earlier people plus blood from the gods. They also believed that they needed to return these ingredients to keep the gods happy.

Return them they did. Each year thousands of prisoners captured in battle were painted yellow, the color of the sun, and killed. Each year a beautiful young man was chosen to personify the sun god. For one year he lived a life worthy of a god. At the end of that year, he was sacrificed on a stone altar by having his heart ripped out with a stone knife.

The sun remained in the sky and continued on its path.

GET THE SLANT ON SUMMER

The reason for seasons is that while the earth travels around the sun, the earth is slanted over on its side. Everybody knows that.

But just try to explain it with words, or even with pictures. You'll find that knowing a fact and knowing how something really works can be two different things.

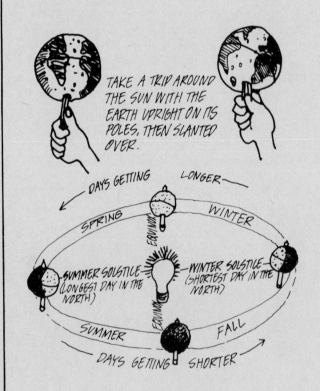

TAKE A TRIP AROUND THE SUN WITH THE EARTH UPRIGHT ON ITS POLES, THEN SLANTED OVER.

DAYS GETTING LONGER

SPRING   EQUINOX   WINTER

SUMMER SOLSTICE (LONGEST DAY IN THE NORTH)   WINTER SOLSTICE (SHORTEST DAY IN THE NORTH)

SUMMER   EQUINOX   FALL

DAYS GETTING SHORTER

Here is an easy way to work it out once and for all:

Get a felt marker, an orange, a pencil, and a lamp (with the shade removed) all in one place.

1. Draw the continents on the orange. (This is a good geography test. See if you can do it without looking at a map.) It might be helpful to dot-in the equator. Use the stem scar as the north pole and the navel as the south pole.

3. Take a spin around the sun. How are the land masses sharing the light?

4. Remove the pencil, and stick it in at a more realistic angle.

5. Take another trip around the sun. How is the light falling on earth now? Can you find summer in North America? Where is winter? How about the equinoxes?

This is your trip around the lamp with an orange, in diagram form. Now maybe all this stuff about longer days, solstices and equinoxes will make more sense. And if it doesn't don't worry about it. It took a long time for the human race to catch on to what was happening in the heavens that made the seasons on earth.

Anyway, you can still eat your orange.

SO HOW COME SUMMER IS HOT?

The easy answer to that is, summer is sunnier. However, it's not quite that simple (it never is, is it?).

During the summer the sun is stronger. The sun is higher in the sky, so the sun's rays are more direct and pass through less atmosphere. This means the rays which reach us are much more concentrated.

You can feel this atmospheric screening effect during the course of one day. Think about how hot the sun can be at high noon. Compare it to that mild afternoon sun that slants in before sunset. It's the same light from our local star all right. The difference in strength is because of miles of atmospheric filter. What's more, during the summer, there are just more hours of light.

But wait a minute. The days are getting shorter. How come the weather is getting hotter?

Right you are. If you take a look at the chart, the days have been getting longer since January. Days have been longer than nights since June. How come it takes so long to get hot?

Glad you asked. It's because of something called the cumulative effect. Or it could be termed the-first-piece-of-toast-takes-forever-but-seconds-take-just-a-flash effect. Both a toaster and the earth's surface take a while to heat up. And to cool down. Heat lag is the reason summer doesn't come sooner.

DOG DAYS

Dog days are those hot, sticky summer days when the only thing happening is flies. Officially dog days happen between early July and early September, or the time when the hottest part of summer is expected. Dog days get their name from the rising of Sirius, called the Dog Star, which is seen on the horizon at this time of year.

USE A FRIEND'S BODY AS A SUN CLOCK. TRACE HIS SHADOW ON THE SIDEWALK WITH A PIECE OF CHALK AT HOUR INTERVALS.

HEY, HOLD STILL

PUNCH A HOLE ABOUT A CENTIMETER WIDE IN A CARD. TAPE IT TO A SOUTH WINDOW. AT NOON MARK THE POSITION OF THIS SPOT OF LIGHT ON THE FLOOR. KEEP TRACK FOR A FEW MONTHS.

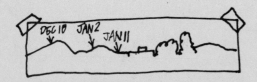

DRAW A PICTURE OR TAKE A PHOTO OF YOUR HORIZON FROM A WEST WINDOW. ABOUT ONCE A WEEK MARK THE SPOT WHERE THE SUN SETS. WHERE DO SOLSTICE DAYS APPEAR ON YOUR HORIZON?

MEASURING COSMIC MOTIONS

You know it's summer because it's hot out. Heat is easy to believe.

On the other hand, it is hard to think of yourself wheeling through the heavens on a dirt earth that tilts its way around a local star. All those cosmic lurches and jerks don't seem connected to you here on earth.

On the left are some simple ways to detect these motions without leaving your backyard.

CATCH THE SUN

Cat's cradle is a traditional Eskimo string game that has magical powers. The native people of the far north would play cat's cradle in order to catch the sun in its meshes and keep it from sinking into the winter sky.

INDIAN SUMMER

Indian Summer is that time of warm, mild weather late in autumn or early in winter often having a hazy sky with no clouds. This idea of Indian Summer is an American one. According to the Oxford dictionary, it seems that Indian Summer happens only in North America. The phrase didn't appear in the English language until 1794. It seems safe to say that Indian Summer is as American as apple pie.

2
SUN POWER

SUN POWER

Our local star burns with ferocious power. Every second, four million tons of sun explode. heat and light into space. Earth gets along powered by a tiny fraction of this energy which happens to pass our way across space.

Even so, our share of the solar rain is more than enough to keep us going here on earth. We get a wide variety of solar energy, some of which we detect as x-rays, radio waves, or ultraviolet rays. The ones that really keep earth life running are the infra-red or heat waves and visible light. If the sun were to suddenly shut down our supply of the solar rain, we would be quite powerless. No need to worry, that doesn't seem likely, at least not for a long while.

Meanwhile earth folks are doing all they can to learn more about sun power and how to put it to work. This chapter shows a lot of ways you can have some fun, and learn about sun power.

AND THERE WAS LIGHT

Light is like nothing else in the universe.

It has the properties of both solid matter in motion and of waves. Sound confusing? It had scientists fooled for centuries.

A radiometer is a simple device that demonstrates that light rays pack a punch. Light rays like to stick to dark surfaces rather than to light ones. So they hit the black sides of the flags on a radiometer harder than the white sides, and it spins. In this case, light rays behave like solid matter.

RADIOMETER

Light waves. We always say it, but what does it mean? A wave is not a solid object, but a form. It is a shape something takes, like waves passing through water or a flag in the wind. Light waves can pass through solid objects like glass. In this case we have to say light acts more like energy than solid matter.

When you come right down to it, we really can't say what light is exactly, although we can predict how it will behave. We can't explain it, but we do know that without it our sort of earth life would be impossible. Light excites our eyes, allowing us to see. It excites our skin and provides us with vitamin D. It excites matter in green plants causing them to produce sugar, which is the basic foodstuff for most earth creatures.

Light is amazing.

SEND AWAY:

SEND AWAY:
RADIOMETER

If you would like a radiometer you should be able to buy one from a place that sells curiousities. Somewhere like a dime store or magic shop. It should cost about $3.00. If you can't find one in a store, you can buy one by mail from the Nature Company. Write to find out how much it will cost to have it sent to your area.

The Nature Company
P. O. Box 7137
Berkeley, California
94707

LIGHT MOBILE

You can make a hanging device that will split light rays and send them bouncing all over the room, decorating everything with bright little bands of color. Mostly what you need is a number of old glass beads. Ones with facets do the best job of breaking up the light.

So dig through your mom's junk jewelry, with her permission of course, and see if you can scrounge up about two dozen beads. Different shapes are better. If you have no luck, try Aunt Annie or a junk store. Stalls at flea markets generally have dishes full of glittery glass beads at giveaway prices. While you're at it, be on the lookout for pieces from old lamps or chandeliers. You will also need some wire and pliers.

Here's how to make a light mobile.

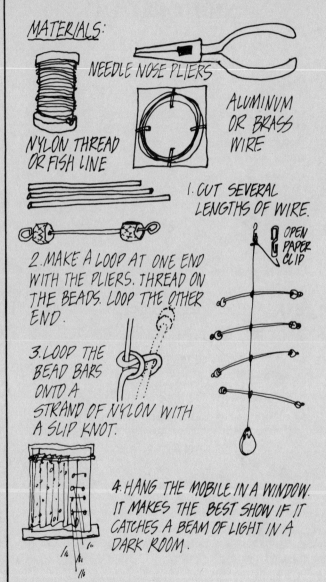

MATERIALS:

NYLON THREAD OR FISH LINE

NEEDLE NOSE PLIERS

ALUMINUM OR BRASS WIRE

1. CUT SEVERAL LENGTHS OF WIRE.

2. MAKE A LOOP AT ONE END WITH THE PLIERS. THREAD ON THE BEADS. LOOP THE OTHER END.

OPEN PAPER CLIP

3. LOOP THE BEAD BARS ONTO A STRAND OF NYLON WITH A SLIP KNOT.

4. HANG THE MOBILE IN A WINDOW. IT MAKES THE BEST SHOW IF IT CATCHES A BEAM OF LIGHT IN A DARK ROOM.

NIGHT AND DAY

Many ancient peoples believed that the sun journeyed through the sky each day, traveling in some sort of vehicle.

The Scandinavians thought the sun moved through the sky in a chariot. When it set, it was said to travel through the dark and dangerous waters of the night. The Greeks also liked to think of the sun traveling across the sky in a chariot.

The Egyptians believed that the sun god traveled across the sky each day in a boat like the ordinary boats that sailed the Nile. Each night it disappeared into the underworld river. Osiris, god of the underworld, had the boat pulled along until it crossed the horizon to continue its eastward journey. Occasionally the great river snake would swallow the boat, causing a solar eclipse.

OBELISK

What would you do if you were unarmed and came face to face with an obelisk?

Freeze until it went away?

Hit it over the head with a rock?

Call the police?

Wrong. You would size it up, then get it tell you the time.

An obelisk is a long, thin thing with a pointy top that sometimes stands in public places. Its job is to cast a shadow by which you can tell the time.

The first obelisks were made by Egyptians to honor their sun god, Ra. They were carved out of a single slab of stone and some were as tall as 100 feet. They were marvels of their time. In fact, engineers today still wonder how the Egyptians managed to raise such stones.

When the Greeks visited Egypt, they too were amazed by these stones. They were so amazed that they called them *obeliskoi* or little spits — sort of like you might call the tallest kid in your class "Shorty."

These Egyptian pillars got around. Today there are ancient Egyptian obelisks in Rome, London, and New York City. The ones in London and New York go by the name of "Cleopatra's Needle." Not all obelisks are from Egypt. You might find a more modern one lurking around a park in your city.

Get it to tell you the time.

ANOTHER SORT OF SUN CLOCK

SUN CLOCK

BEAD PLACED AT ONE END

MARK THE BEAD'S SHADOW AT EACH NEW HOUR.

X X X
12 11 10 9

N W S E

NORTH-SOUTH POSITION

You can make this sundial from a round box, like the kind oatmeal comes in, or a large mailing tube. All you need is a string, some tape, and a bit of cardboard.

1. Cut the box or tube in half. Cut the lid as well.

2. Tape the lid to the box.

3. Cut two rectangles from stiff card or poster board. They should be exactly the same size.

4. Thread a small bead to the center of the string. Tie it in the center; or you can tie a fat knot in the string if you don't have a bead.

5. Tape the string in place.

6. Glue or tape the rectangles to either end of the sun clock.

Place it out in the sun so that the string lines up in a north-south position. Every hour mark the spot where the knot's shadow shows. Grad-ually, the spots will shift. You might try different colored markings for different months.

P. S. This is not the most weatherproof of sun clocks. Don't forget to bring it in when it rains. Also warn your mom about its where-abouts, so she doesn't accidently water it.

SEND AWAY:

TIME SHEET

How would you like a whole poster full of moon faces, a whole months worth? What if the back side of the poster was filled with a sur-prising photo of what happens when a bullet rips through a series of balloons, plus some other shots of "frozen moments"? You can get both of these posters plus a leaflet that will give you some ideas for studying moments and cycles or, in short, the stuff of time. All of this costs $1.25. Learning Magazine calls them study prints. They are written for teachers, but kids can use them too. Write for a Time Study Print. Send your request to:

Starting Points
530 University Avenue
Palo Alto, California
94301

SEND AWAY:

ENERGY ACTIVITY GUIDE

Did you know that our ancestors used about 2000 calories of energy per day? Today in the

USA each person uses the equivalent of about 230,000 calories per day. This extra energy is due to heating, lighting, transportation, and the manufacturing of the things we use. What's more, our energy appetite shows no sign of slowing down.

There is a 28 page booklet that is full of all sorts of ways to get you thinking about energy. There is the sad saga of fossil fuel, a key to energy sources, energy equivalents (did you know that in a month your TV uses something more than a gallon of gas?), and how to make an energy budget. It's colorful, it's lively, and it's free, from:

Project On Energy
National Recreation and Park Association
1601 North Kent Street
Arlington, Virginia
22209

SOLAR COOKER

Life on our planet is made out of proteins. High heat destroys proteins. It is no lucky accident that our sun is a nice, safe distance away to keep us comfortably warm. A few million miles closer, and we would all cook to death. On earth, life evolved specially fitted to live at this distance from the sun — a comfy 93,000,000 miles.

When you make a solar cooker, you have a problem to solve. That is, how to turn a normally friendly environment for proteins into one that will cook them.

Since you can't turn up the sun, your only solution is to collect a lot of light and focus it in one spot. This concentrated spot of energy should cook things in no time.

COOKING PAPER

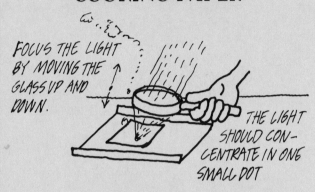

FOCUS THE LIGHT BY MOVING THE GLASS UP AND DOWN.

THE LIGHT SHOULD CONCENTRATE IN ONE SMALL DOT

The simplest demonstration of the power packed by a dot of concentrated sunlight is the old magnifying-glass trick. On a sunny day you can burn a hole through a piece of paper in just a few seconds with a good magnifying glass.

1. Adjust the magnifier and the paper so the spot of light is as small as you can get it. Do this on the cement or on a metal tray so you don't start a fire or burn a hole in the furniture or floor. The more light you can collect and focus, the hotter the spot will get. There is a famous solar furnace in the French Pyrenees that collects light from 7/10 of an acre of mirrors (an area equal to the size of about half of a football field). It gets as hot as 6,735 degrees Fahrenheit. Hot enough to burn a hole through just about anything on earth.

LIGHT CEREMONY

Collecting light to start fires is not a new idea. In some parts of the world it has had a religious meaning.

Before the Europeans came to this continent, the Incas worshipped the sun. Once a year the high priest led a procession into the city of Cuzco. Each year he focused the sun's rays, using a bronze mirror, onto a ball of cotton. A white llama was sacrificed and burned in these flames as an offering to the sun. All year these sacred flames were tended until three days before solstice. Then they were snuffed out in order to make ready for the new year's ceremony.

EGGS ON THE SIDEWALK

Probably you have never thought of the sidewalk as a solar cooker. Well it can be. Remember the expression "it's hot enough to fry an egg on the sidewalk"? It can be done. Sidewalks have a way of collecting and holding the sun's heat energy, getting hot enough to cook proteins. You will need 144 degrees to get eggs to thicken. Try the experiments in the next section to find out the best way to turn your sidewalk into a solar cooker.

SEE HOW THE COLOR BLACK AND A GLASS HELP TRAP HEAT.

BLACK FRY PAN.

BLACK PAN COVERED WITH GLASS

EGG ON THE OPEN SIDEWALK.

PARABOLIC COOKER

To make the cooker, catch some sunlight with some very shiny material. Then you have to form this reflector material into a shape that will focus the sun's rays into a small area. If you can do this, you will have a contraption that will cook a couple of hot dogs or some shish kabobs in about 15 minutes.

SEND AWAY:
SUN SHOWER

The Ecology Center has a sheet that tells how to make a simple solar shower. It is a project that would require a large drum and plenty of adult help, but the idea is very straightforward. If you are interested write:

The Ecology Center
2179 Allston Way
Berkeley, California
94704

Include a stamped, self-addressed envelope.

GUM WRAPPER THERMOMETER

You can make this little machine to tell temperatures with junk from around the house. All you need is a spool, some tape, and some of the silver paper that comes wrapped around gum.

<u>MATERIALS:</u>
YOU WILL NEED SOME CARDBOARD, A WIRE COAT HANGER, A SHEET OF MYLAR OR ACETATE WITH A SILVER COATING. (YOU CAN GET THESE FROM AN ART SUPPLY STORE)

1. TRACE THE SHAPE ON THIS PAGE ONTO A PIECE OF PAPER. CUT IT OUT AS SHOWN.

2. CUT OUT 4 OF THESE SHAPES FROM CARD-BOARD. MAKE THEM EXACT.

3. GLUE THEM TO-GETHER INTO TWO SETS. LET THEM DRY.

4. CUT THE ACETATE INTO A PIECE MEASURING 13" X 16". CUT A PIECE OF CARDBOARD THE SAME SIZE.

5. PUT STRIPS OF MASKING TAPE ALONG THE EDGES. SNIP AT 1" INTERVALS.

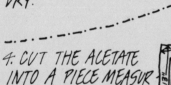

CORRUGATIONS CROSSWISE

16"

SNIP TO MYLAR

ONE-INCH MASKING TAPE

<u>ASSEMBLE:</u>

6. CAREFULLY STICK THE MYLAR TO THE CARDBOARD ENDS.

7. ATTACH THE CARDBOARD THE SAME WAY, ON TOP OF THE MYLAR.

8. HOLD IT UP TO DIRECT SUN-LIGHT. STICK A PIECE OF COAT HANGER THROUGH AT THE SPOT WHERE THE LIGHT FOCUSES.

<u>TO COOK</u>
TO GET ENOUGH HEAT YOU MAY HAVE TO WRAP THE FOOD IN SOLAR FOIL. MAKE SOME BY PAINTING ONE SIDE OF ALUMINUM FOIL BLACK. IT CAN BE RECYCLED.

HOT DOG

OUTSIDE

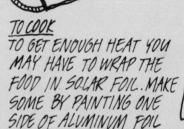

PLACE THE COOKER IN DIRECT SUNLIGHT OUT OF THE WIND. MAKE SURE IT IS WELL FOCUSED.

BOY, WHAT A DUMB THERMO-
METER. IT DOESN'T HAVE
ANY DEGREES

FOIL STRIP

METAL STRIP

TAPE

HOT

COLD

PAPER STRIP

WHEN METAL GETS HOT IT EXPANDS, GETTING
LONGER AND WIDER. A CURVED SHAPE LETS
THE TWO STRIPS STAY TOGETHER WITH THE
METAL ARC TAKING MORE ROOM.

1. Cut a pointer from the gum wrapper. (Make sure the wrapper is the kind with foil on one side and paper on the other.)

2. Tape it to the spool. Anything like a little bottle or a felt marker will work.

3. Set it on a paper and mark where the pointer is. Watch the needle swing around when the temperature changes.

I forgot to tell you that this thermometer doesn't tell you how hot it is. It just tells you if it's hotter than it was. But you already knew it was hot.

Think about bi-metal strips for a moment. (It will take your mind off the heat.) The reason this little device works is that the pointer is made of two different materials. Paper and metal foil don't react the same way when exposed to the same amount of heat. The foil expands at a much faster rate than the paper. The difference is shown.

The thermostat in your house works on the same principle. It keeps track of the temperature by expanding and contracting.

TAN

In a way the air, dust, and clouds that blanket our earth make up our first layer of skin. Without this shield, much of the sun's radiation would promptly kill most things that live and breathe on this earth.

Even so, this blanket protection is not quite enough. Some ultraviolet rays still get through. These are the ones that the suntan oil companies call "harmful, burning rays." These rays are able to destroy skin cells result-

SKIN COMES IN LAYERS, SORT OF LIKE A
CAKE. THE TANNING PART IS JUST UNDER
THE DEAD OUTER LAYER. IT IS A GRAINY
SUBSTANCE INSIDE THE CELLS CALLED
MELANIN.

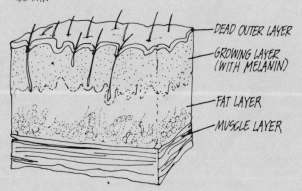

DEAD OUTER LAYER

GROWING LAYER
(WITH MELANIN)

FAT LAYER

MUSCLE LAYER

ing in serious burns. Not only that, outdoor types like lifeguards and farmers are more prone to develop skin cancer.

However, your skin doesn't take a beating from the sun lying down. It makes *melanin* (MEL ah nin). Melanin is a substance in skin cells that is able to soak up ultra-violet light, preventing harm. It is a protective color umbrella, screening your insides from the sun. Some people carry a lot of melanin around with them all the time. Dark-skinned people have a kind of full time sun insurance. Some people have very little melanin. They are the pale ones that burn easily in the sun. Some light-skinned people have the ability to turn darker when their skin is exposed to the sun. Their skin cells have grains of melanin that develop on contact with sunlight — they "tan."

SUNSHINE VITAMIN

Sunlight is beneficial. Ever hear of the sunshine vitamin? Sunlight is able to cause a chemical change which converts a substance in your skin to vitamin D.

Vitamin D is necessary for proper bone growth and it is rare in the human diet (unless you eat polar bear liver). Since man grew up in the earth's sunny spots, vitamin D was as easy as a sun bath. But when humans began moving away from the sunny countries into the northern countries, sunlight got a little scarce, especially in the wintertime. Skin became lighter to let in more of the beneficial effects. Even today, you can see a paling of hides as you move away from the equator.

Rickets, a bone formation disease, was common in northern countries — especially for children born in winter — until science discovered cod-liver oil. Yucky, awful stuff made from — you guessed it — ground up fish livers. Now even kids in the north countries don't need to worry. Milk and bread are treated so they contain about all the vitamin D you need. And if you live in Florida, you never need to worry.

FRECKLES

Now that you know all about suntan, you are probably curious about freckles, especially you readers with red hair.

Freckles are sun glops of melanin color in your skin.

Most people have their melanin color evenly spread through the middle layer of their skin.

People with freckles have glops of melanin. Sometimes these don't show until they are exposed to sunlight. Some people have skin so light that their freckles stay all year long.

P. S. A freckled person should be sure to put suntan oil between freckles where their natural sun screen is thin.

SUNTAN OIL

You can whip up your own suntan oil. All you need is some light oil, like sesame or baby oil, and some tea bags. Tea bags contain tannins that provide the sunscreen action. This oil should block up to 50% of the sun's burning rays. Very sensitive skins will need more protection.

TEST SOME OF THE SUNTAN OIL ON YOUR SKIN FOR A SHORT TIME BEFORE STAYING OUT ALL DAY.

1. Pour 1/3 cup of boiling water over two tea bags. Let them steep until the water is dark.

2. Pour 1/4 cup of oil into a pan or blender.

3. Add the tea to the oil and blend or beat until the liquids are mixed.

4. Keep the suntan oil in a bottle. Shake well before using.

SUNGLASSES

Sometimes people call them "shades" which is a good way to describe these spectacles made for blocking out some of the sun's rays.

Shades work a couple of ways. Some block out light according to color. Somebody who looks at the world through rose-colored glasses, has on glasses that filter out everything but red rays.

Polarized shades block out all light except that from a certain direction. Light, in the natural world, bounces off beaches and shiny surfaces. It is scattered in all directions as it comes pouring through the atmosphere. A favorite way to explain a polarized filter is to pretend that it is like a picket fence. Light waves are like a jump rope being wiggled through the slots in the fence.

Only the up and down wiggles will make it through the fence-filter; the sidewise ones won't.

The oldest sort of sunglasses are the kind that just block the light, letting in only slits of light through an opaque material. Eskimos fashioned this sort from bone to prevent snow blindness. Follow the instructions to make your own cardboard version.

HOMEMADE SHADES

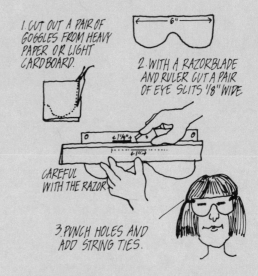

1. CUT OUT A PAIR OF GOGGLES FROM HEAVY PAPER OR LIGHT CARDBOARD.

2. WITH A RAZORBLADE AND RULER CUT A PAIR OF EYE SLITS 1/8" WIDE

CAREFUL WITH THE RAZOR

3. PUNCH HOLES AND ADD STRING TIES.

SUN-RAY PROJECTIONS

Artists have always been interested in light. Artists have pictured their subjects in candlelight or with strong spotlight effects. The impressionists tried to paint the sunlit atmosphere. Photographers use the light to make pictures. Computer artists draw with something called a light pen.

SUN-RAY PROJECTIONS

CHANGE A BEAM OF LIGHT COMING INTO YOUR ROOM INTO A PATTERN YOU CAN REFLECT ON THE WALLS OR ON THE CEILING. LOOK AROUND THE HOUSE FOR REFLECTORS, PRISMS, LENSES, FILTERS. WHATEVER CHANGES THE PATH OF LIGHT.

THE BEST LIGHT SHOWS HAPPEN IN DARK ROOMS WITH WHITE WALLS.

VERY SHINY METAL OBJECTS ARE GOOD REFLECTORS

SHAVING MIRROR

PRISM

CELLOPHANE

COLORED FILTERS. TAPE THEM TO A WINDOW

MIRRORS OF ALL SHAPES. OLD COMPACTS ARE GOOD.

ALUMINUM AND COLORED FOILS.

COMBED LIGHT

COMB

CARDBOARD WITH HOLE

MIRROR REFLECTOR.

RAINBOWS

MAKE A LIQUID PRISM:

MIRROR SET AT AN ANGLE.

ICE CUBE TRAY WITH WATER

A GLASS WITH ANGLED SIDES SPLITS LIGHT INTO PRISM COLORS.

WATER

MIRROR BALL

BITS OF BROKEN MIRROR GLUED ON AN OLD TENNIS BALL. SUSPEND IT FROM A STRING.

Here is a new way to be an artist with light. You can make light projections on the wall or ceiling of your room. You can create many interesting effects, and best of all, erase it in a flash.

This is a good thing to do indoors on a hot afternoon when it's scorching outside. Assemble your equipment, slink off to your room, and let in just a chink of light.

SEND AWAY:
LIGHT TOOLS

The Lawrence Hall of Science at the University of California will send you a free catalog of good cheap tools for exploring with. They sell a sun print kit that lets you make light pictures using water as a fixer. They also sell prisms, magnifiers, and kits you can build that are working models of old astronomers' tools.

Write to:

Discovery Corner
Lawrence Hall of Science
University of California
Berkeley, California
94720

PICTURES
FROM LIGHT

You can make pictures on photographic paper without a camera, using the power of sunlight. This sort of picture is called a photogram.

To do this you will need some special things from the camera store:

a package of studio proof paper (or contact printing paper, as it is sometimes called)
a box of fixer (sodium thiosulfate)
a sheet of clear glass
a glass or plastic pan bigger than your paper (8x10 inches)
a piece of cardboard

1. First mix up the fixer. ¼ cup crystals plus 2 cups hot water should be enough. Stir to dissolve them. Let it cool. Pour it into the pan when you are ready.

2. If you want to do some samples first, cut some sheets of paper into quarters. Do this inside away from direct light. Keep the photo paper in its little, black envelope until you are ready to use it. It's sensitive stuff.

3. Find something to print. A leaf or piece of grass should do nicely for a trial run.

4. Place the photo paper on the cardboard. Put the leaf on the piece of photo paper. Put the glass on top, to hold it in place.

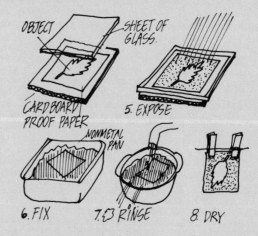
OBJECT   SHEET OF GLASS.
CARD BOARD PROOF PAPER   5. EXPOSE
6. FIX   NONMETAL PAN   7. RINSE   8. DRY

5. Expose this sandwich to light until it turns dark purple.

6. Move it into the shade. Remove the paper and drop it in the fixer. Swish it around for about 2 minutes.

7. Wash in running water for 10-15 minutes.

8. Hang it up to dry for about 2 hours.

9. When still slightly damp, flatten the photogram under a couple of hefty books, like the encyclopedia.

HIGH-NOON PORTRAITS

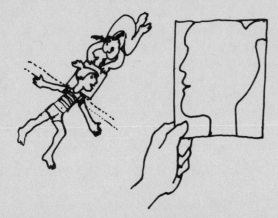

Whenever there is strong sunlight, the conditions are right for high noon portraits. Grab a friend, a pen, a paper; hold still and get traced. Write a letter on the back and send it to grandma. She'll love it.

The best time to do this is when the sun is either low or high in the sky. At noon you can put your paper flat on the ground. In the early morning or late day tape it up onto a smooth wall.

1. Put the paper so that the person's profile falls on to it (make sure the paper is big enough).

2. Trace around the shadow with a felt marker. Try to make the line smooth.

3. Trade around and have your friend trace yours.

PORTRAIT STUDIO

Take your tracing a step further and turn it into a photogram, suitable for framing. You will need the same materials as for photograms: studio proof paper and fixer.

1. Cut out your silhouette along the lines you traced. Now is your chance to smooth out those squiggle lines, but be careful. It's the little variations that make the portrait.

2. Turn it into a photogram using the directions on page 29.

Remember, you can make lots of copies from one paper silhouette. You could do all the kids on the block. Charge 25 cents a head or three for 50 cents — in case both their grandmas want one.

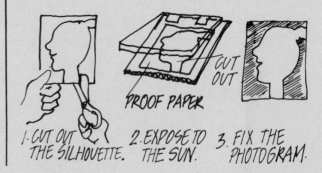

1. CUT OUT THE SILHOUETTE.   2. EXPOSE TO THE SUN.   3. FIX THE PHOTOGRAM.

3

KEEP COOL

HOT-BLOODED

Pound-for-pound, your body produces more heat than the sun. But because the sun is so much more dense than you are, it is able to produce great amounts of heat. Still, your body — and every mammal's — is pretty hot stuff.

Here's how your body loses heat:

EVAPORATION 25%
SWEAT TURNS TO GAS
VAPOR ON YOUR SKIN

RADIATION 60%
ALL OBJECTS HOTTER
THAN THEIR SUR-
ROUNDINGS
LOSE HEAT,
LIKE COALS
IN A FIRE.

CONVECTION 12%
TINY WINDS
CAUSED BY HOT
SKIN CAUSE
EXTRA EVAPOR-
ATION

CONDUCTION - 3% - THIS IS HEAT LOST THROUGH
ONE OBJECT TOUCHING A COOLER OBJECT. LIKE
A POT ON A HOT PLATE OR FEET ON A COLD FLOOR.

FORTUNETELLING FISH

What is a magic trick doing in this section on keeping cool?

This trick works because of your cooling system. The heat from your palm causes cellophane to curl. So the cellophane fish flips his tail to tell your fortune. That's the "magic," but a magician need not divulge all his secrets.

To make a fortunetelling fish, you will need a small piece of cellophane. Cigarette packs and some sorts of bread come wrapped in cellophane. Sometimes it's hard to tell it from plastic. But you'll know the difference, because no matter how sweaty your palm is, plastic won't curl. Plastic fish won't tell fortunes.

1. Lay the cellophane over this picture.

2. Trace the fish onto the cellophane. India ink or certain felt markers will draw on cellophane.

3. Cut out the fish.

To tell a fortune: place the fish flat on somebody's palm. If the tail curls it means:

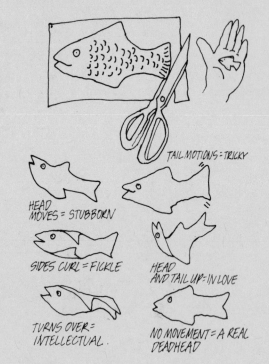

TAIL MOTIONS = TRICKY

HEAD
MOVES = STUBBORN

SIDES CURL = FICKLE

HEAD
AND TAIL UP = IN LOVE

TURNS OVER =
INTELLECTUAL.

NO MOVEMENT = A REAL
DEADHEAD

YOUR TEMPERATURE CONTROL

Your body likes its inside temperature at a nice warm 98 degrees Fahrenheit. Usually the air temperature is lower than your body temperature. Your body's problem is keeping you warm. Your muscle action, plus some insulation from fat and clothing, do the job.

When the air temperature climbs in summer to equal the temperature of your insides, things can get dangerously hot inside your body. That's when your body's cooling system goes into action.

As much as 1/3 of your hot blood can be sent through the tiny blood vessels just under your skin where it can be cooled by radiation, conduction, and convection. However, when the temperature outside equals or tops that of your insides, these methods just can't do the whole job. Something more must be done. That's when evaporation steps in.

Evaporation can be described as the process that changes your soggy wet, just washed socks to dry ones on the clothesline. When evaporation happens, liquid changes to gas; the water disappears from your socks into the air. Evaporation is accompanied by a drop in temperature. Anybody who has ever worn damp socks can tell you that.

Your body depends on the evaporation process to keep it cool on hot days. Water flows onto your skin through millions of sweat pores. As the water evaporates, you are cooled. Usually you don't notice this, even though you sweat all of the time. But on sizzling summer days, or after a sprint around the block, your body pours it on.

The next section is an experiment to prove how evaporation makes a body cool.

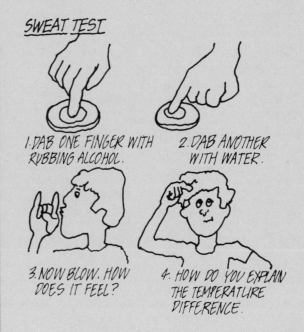

SWEAT TEST

1. DAB ONE FINGER WITH RUBBING ALCOHOL.

2. DAB ANOTHER WITH WATER.

3. NOW BLOW. HOW DOES IT FEEL?

4. HOW DO YOU EXPLAIN THE TEMPERATURE DIFFERENCE.

THE ICKY STICKIES

How much heat can the human take? As it turns out, quite a lot. Humans can survive several hours at 200 degrees Fahrenheit with no serious effects, *provided it's heat in a dry environment.*

In very humid places it's another story. Our inside temperatures begin to rise when it gets to

be 94 degrees outside. And that's sitting still.
When the body is at work, the limit is lowered to
85 degrees.

High humidity throws a wrench in your
body's cooling system. Air can absorb a limited
amount of water. On highly humid days the
air has close to its fill of water. Sweat stacks up
on your skin taking much longer to be absorbed
into the air. Your cooling system has slowed
way down. You feel hot and sticky.

FAN THEORY

When we sit still, the air touching our bodies gets humid. If you find this hard to believe,

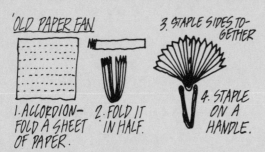

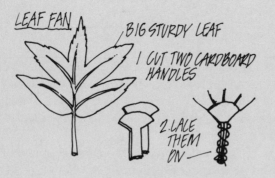

remember how damp your feet get in rubber
boots.

This is especially true on hot days when
your cooling system is going full blast. You
can help keep yourself cool by moving the air
around, trading the sweaty, close air for air
that's farther away.

In other words, you need a breeze. These
are some hand-powered machines you can make
to create a breeze. They go by the name of fans.

KEEPING COOL:
LESSONS FROM
THE ANIMAL KINGDOM

Wet your feathers. Keeping your body covering damp can bring your temperature way down.

Noontime siesta and moving at night. This
helps to take advantage of the cool times. Most
desert dwellers are active at night or during the
dawn and dusk hours. Midday is the time to rest.

Find a rock and crawl under it. In the scorching desert, reptiles survive by finding or digging their own microclimate. Where is the coolest spot around your place?

Increase your surface area. Spreading out, so that none of your parts touch, increases your surface area. This way more air can circulate and cool you. Compare this to how you might sit while ice fishing.

Wallow in the mud. This can do a lot to keep you cool. For many animals it has the added attraction of leaving a coat that protects from nasty bites.

Showers keep you cool.

Stay in the shade. Especially under trees. Have you ever noticed how animals stay under trees on a hot day? They know they are shielded from the sun's rays. Also, it's cooler because of what's called "transpiration." Trees breathe out carbon dioxide and water. Underneath it you feel a tree's cool breath.

Panting. There are many furry mammals that have no sweat glands. Their bodies are cooled by passing air over their lungs. Lots of air. They pant.

Don't move a muscle. Muscle activity creates heat. So keep still and keep cool.

A BODY OF WATER

Have you ever thought about how wet you are inside? No? Think about it now.

Take a survey:

Run your tongue around the inside of your mouth.

Stick a finger in your nose and your eyes.

Breathe out on your fingers.

Think about your last trip to the bathroom.

What happens when you cut a finger?

Your insides are damp indeed. You might say water is your most important substance. If you think in percentages, your body is about 60 percent water.

We are water creatures who live on dry land; only we carry our oceans around inside of us. Our inside oceans get used up. We lose a little water with every breath. It gets poured out on skin to keep us cool. It helps flush wastes out of our system in the form of urine.

Bodies are affected greatly by the loss of water. When one percent of a body's water is lost, the person gets thirsty. When five percent is lost the person collapses. Ten percent loss of water causes death.

Water must be put back into the body, so drink up, especially in sweaty old summer.

FOR A 50 LB. KID 1% OF HIS BODY WEIGHT EQUALS 1/2 A LB. OR AN 8 OZ. GLASS OF WATER.

THIRST = OR 1/2 LB WATER

COLLAPSE = OR 2 1/2 LBS. WATER

DEATH = OR 5 LBS. WATER

DESERT-SUN TEA

You don't have to live in the desert to brew desert-sun tea. You just need a sunny day and some patience.

Gather together in the morning:

A quart-sized clean glass jar or bottle with a lid

Two tea bags

1. Fill the jar or bottle with cool water, then add tea bags. Leave bag strings sticking out and screw top on.

2. Put jar or bottle in a sunny place outside for three or so hours. The water will be heated from the sun to brew the tea.

3. When it's ready, take out the tea bags and add some crushed mint leaves, if you like. Put the jar in the refrigerator to cool it. Pour cold tea over ice and add sugar and lemon.

MICROCLIMATE

Just by climbing a stalk of grass, an insect can choose from a warm and sunny or a cool and moist climate.

A desert rat can escape the searing 160 degree temperatures of the desert surface by burrowing underground. In fact, a journey from the ground to a foot and a half above ground can be like a trip from sub-tropical to sub-polar regions.

The name for this quick change of conditions is microclimate. Microclimates are many and not far between.

A lot of creatures carry their own microclimates around with them, in the form of shells, fur, or feathers. Sheep wear their microclimates as fleece. Scientists tested some merino sheep in Australia. The surface of their wool was too hot to handle. However, the woolly depths below the surface were 60-70 degrees lower than their surface temperature. So you can stop feeling sorry for a woolly sheep on a hot day.

Next to its shorn comrades, a fully dressed sheep breathes only half as fast. Panting is a sure sign of a hot sheep. Fleecing a sheep is like stealing its microclimate.

Our own human species has become a masterful manipulator of microclimates. Man has been described as a tropical animal that takes his climate with him in the form of clothes. Clothing makes it possible for him to survive in The Arctic and the Sahara. Given the proper cover, there's no corner on the surface of the earth where man hasn't been.

DRESSING FOR HOT

Oddly enough, within the tropics — the earth's hot spot — there are two approaches to dress. The Dinkas of Sudan wear nothing, while the Arabs of the Sahara wear a lot of loose-fitting white clothing.

Probably pale, North European type persons have no choice. They need some shield from the sun or they would be scorched. Clothing provides this, plus a zone of air next to the skin which forms insulation. After a time, sweat will dampen this zone and the clothing next to it. The holes in the cloth will fill with water which is a very efficient heat conductor. Heat is lost 5 to 20 times faster in damp clothes than in dry ones. So putting clothes on — provided they have lots of holes for "breathing" space — should keep you cooler. Sounds weird, but it works.

GET A HAT

Too much sun can be a dangerous thing. If you think of sunlight as a sort of daily shower of radiant energy that rains down on earth, you would be less likely to give yourself an overdose of it.

One place that is very sensitive to heat is the top of your head. Brain proteins are quite unstable at even slightly raised temperatures. And being right up there on top of everything, your skull gets the sun full force.

Peoples of the hot, tropical regions have a bit of natural protection. Their fluffy hair gives them insulation from the sun in the same way that a woolly sheep stays cool.

The next best sort of protection against frying your brains is a hat. If you're lost in the desert, or mowing lawns this summer, or sitting in a stadium watching a ball game, a hat is a good idea. In fact, people who spend time out in the sun anywhere in the world know the value of a hat.

COOLIE HAT

This one is a genuine copy of the Chinese coolie hat, which is popular headwear for millions of people in the world. Usually a coolie hat is woven out of grasses. This one also is made of plant stuff. See if you can figure out where the makings for this hat come from.

Makings:
cardboard (grocery box weight or thinner)
string
a needle to thread the string through
a heavy-duty pair of scissors
a large nail for punching holes
a ruler and a pencil

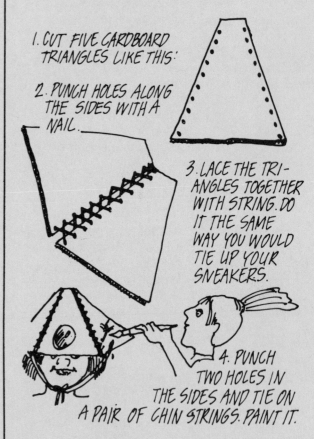

1. CUT FIVE CARDBOARD TRIANGLES LIKE THIS:

2. PUNCH HOLES ALONG THE SIDES WITH A NAIL.

3. LACE THE TRIANGLES TOGETHER WITH STRING. DO IT THE SAME WAY YOU WOULD TIE UP YOUR SNEAKERS.

4. PUNCH TWO HOLES IN THE SIDES AND TIE ON A PAIR OF CHIN STRINGS. PAINT IT.

FOLD-UP HATS

Here are some fold-up hats you can make in an emergency.

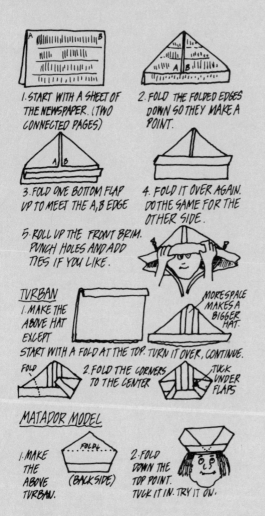

1. START WITH A SHEET OF THE NEWSPAPER. (TWO CONNECTED PAGES)

2. FOLD THE FOLDED EDGES DOWN SO THEY MAKE A POINT.

3. FOLD ONE BOTTOM FLAP UP TO MEET THE A,B EDGE

4. FOLD IT OVER AGAIN. DO THE SAME FOR THE OTHER SIDE.

5. ROLL UP THE FRONT BRIM. PUNCH HOLES AND ADD TIES IF YOU LIKE.

TURBAN
1. MAKE THE ABOVE HAT EXCEPT

MORE SPACE MAKES A BIGGER HAT.

START WITH A FOLD AT THE TOP. TURN IT OVER, CONTINUE.

FOLD

2. FOLD THE CORNERS TO THE CENTER

TUCK UNDER FLAPS

MATADOR MODEL

1. MAKE THE ABOVE TURBAN.

FOLD (BACKSIDE)

2. FOLD DOWN THE TOP POINT. TUCK IT IN. TRY IT ON.

WATER PLAY

The best way to keep cool in the summer is to get wet. However, not everybody is lucky enough to live near a swimming place. Don't let that stop you. You can still get soaking wet and have a great time, if you have a garden hose and a patch of grass. The next section shows how.

WATER GARDEN

If your house is surrounded by a lawn, you probably already have a good assortment of little machines that turn water into sculpture. They are called sprinklers.

Ask where the grass needs soaking, and set up shop. You can turn the lawn into a water garden by setting up a number of sprinklers. If you have more than one hose, you can make water arches, fountains, bridges, and columns. Use your imagination, but most of all, get wet.

If your mom or dad is in the market for a new sprinkler, you might go along to the garden shop and help pick one out. You will be amazed at the variety of devices that somebody has thought up to make water leap, squirt, and squiggle around. While sprinklers are not

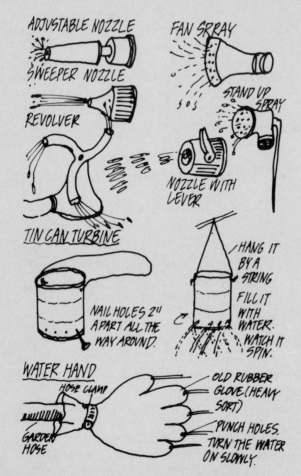

ADJUSTABLE NOZZLE

SWEEPER NOZZLE

REVOLVER

FAN SPRAY

STAND UP SPRAY

NOZZLE WITH LEVER

TIN CAN TURBINE

NAIL HOLES 2" APART ALL THE WAY AROUND.

HANG IT BY A STRING

FILL IT WITH WATER.

WATCH IT SPIN.

WATER HAND

HOSE CLAMP

GARDEN HOSE

OLD RUBBER GLOVE (HEAVY SORT)

PUNCH HOLES. TURN THE WATER ON SLOWLY.

something you would want to spend your allowance on, you could cast some deciding votes in favor of a new piece for your water sculpture.

WATER WHIP

Here is a wild water toy you can set up in your backyard. When you turn on the faucet it seems to take on a life of its own, thrashing about and throwing a stream of water in every direction.

You will need a garden hose (the softer and more flexible, the better), some wire or fabric ties, a stake (an old broom handle works fine), and a nozzle. There are a lot of different kinds of nozzles to choose from. A lightweight plastic kind is best for two reasons: one, a lightweight nozzle will give you the most action; two, a heavy metal one can give you an uncomfortable thunk on the head as it whips around. There are a variety of plastic ones. Check your local garden supply shop.

To set up the water whip:

1. Find an open grassy area.

2. Drive the broom handle into the ground so it is solid. You might need some adult help here.

3. Tie the hose with nozzle attached to the stake. Leave about two feet free at the end.

4. Now turn the water on. Adjust the length of the hose and the water pressure until your water whip begins to behave like a wild animal.

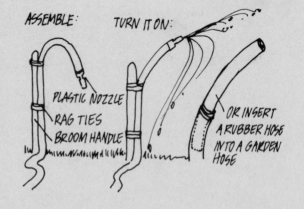

ASSEMBLE: TURN IT ON:

PLASTIC NOZZLE

RAG TIES

BROOM HANDLE

OR INSERT A RUBBER HOSE INTO A GARDEN HOSE

WATER SLIDE

Water slides are a good time, and guaranteed to keep you cool even on the hottest days, while you're running and jumping and having a good old time.

You need at least a ten-foot length of plastic tarp and a grassy spot to put it down on, with a bit of extra room for a runway. Also you will need a hose with a sprinkler.

A plastic tarp can be gotten at the paint or hardware store. You can buy a big 20 foot by 20 foot square for about 89 cents. These tend to be rather thin. They have about half an hour of good slides in them before they get ripped by toenails and elbows. It is better to buy about six yards of heavier plastic off a roll. It will cost more, but you can use it for many summers.

How to do it:

1. Set the plastic tarp up in a place free of lumps and bumps.

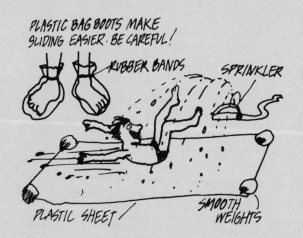

PLASTIC BAG BOOTS MAKE SLIDING EASIER · BE CAREFUL!

RUBBER BANDS

SPRINKLER

PLASTIC SHEET

SMOOTH WEIGHTS

2. Secure the ends with smooth stones or objects that won't leave scratches if you crash into them.

3. Set up a sprinkler so that it keeps the surface wet and slick. When it is, you can test out the slide.

4. Experiment around to see what makes the best slide. You might want to try some plastic-bag boots.

P. S. Don't leave the tarp on the lawn for more than about 30 minutes. The combination of wear and the heat that builds up under the plastic has a way of assassinating large patches of lawn.

HOW TO MAKE RAINBOWS

While you're out playing with the hose, you might see a rainbow. If you're very observant, you know that rainbows happen only under special conditions.

Wild rainbows happen when the air is filled with spherical water droplets and the sky behind the rainbow is hazy or cloudy. Then the sun comes out behind you. This is when a wild rainbow will make an appearance at a place in the sky about halfway between the horizon and a point straight up in the sky.

You can make a rainbow if you can duplicate these conditions.

1. You need to fill the air with a fine misty spray.

2. The sun needs to be behind you.

3. Move around so that your eye looks at the mist at about a 45-degree angle. You will know when you have your eye in this position, because you will see rainbow colors.

COLORFUL FACTS

Drops of water in the air act like many tiny prisms, splitting white light into its spectral colors.

Bigger droplets cause brighter colors. Summer thunder storms are often followed by bright rainbows.

People who fly have reported circular rainbows. Do you have any idea why this might happen?

SEND AWAY:

CAPTAIN HYDRO

Captain Hydro is a kind of a weird dude. After all, how many heroes shout "holy hydraulics" when confronted with grave danger? Besides battling the evil water bandit, Captain Hydro has a lot to say about water. You can find out how to make a rain gauge and how to experiment with soil erosion. Plus, there are puzzles and problems to make you waterwise.

If you don't get your water from East Bay M. U. D. of California, you can get your Captain Hydro comic by sending 25 cents to:

East Bay Municipal Utility District
P. O. Box 24055
Oakland, California
94623

Kids and teachers in the San Francisco area's East Bay can get copies at their local water office. P. S. Where do you get your water?

WATER WAR

This is a good thing to do on the last day of camp, especially if it is a hot day. Everybody — adults too — brings their favorite water weapons like squirt guns, balloons for water bombs, and plastic buckets. Come dressed to get wet. Water wars are best as the last event of the day.

Draw up some boundaries. Try to play in an area big enough for sneaking around and ambushes. Stay outside. Mark off a safe zone; anybody in this spot is to be left high and dry, and no fair shooting from the safe zone.

When the water war begins, it's every man for himself. The whole point is to get wet and have a good time. That's not to say you can't aim for the rotten kid who put ants in your lunch. It's over when everyone is drenched and too tired to go on. Don't forget the towels.

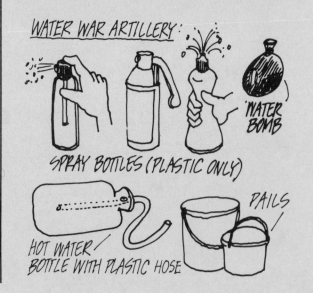

WATER WAR ARTILLERY:

'WATER BOMB

SPRAY BOTTLES (PLASTIC ONLY)

HOT WATER BOTTLE WITH PLASTIC HOSE

PAILS

WATER

The project before this one told you how to throw water around for fun. It's good stuff for bringing down your temperature. It's the home of trout and the lifeblood of the farm business. It's what you wash your dishes with. It is the fluid that keeps you alive. Water is much too important to take for granted.

You can learn a lot about water and water pollution from a Ranger Rick reprint called "Water — What Would We Do Without It?" It has a section on water projects and questions you can use to study this runny stuff. One copy is free. Additional copies are 15 cents from:

Educational Servicing
National Wildlife Federation
1412 16th Street, N. W.
Washington, D. C.
20036

ICE CREAM

Rich Romans ate ice cream. Runners brought snow down from the mountains. Then it was flavored with the juice of fruits. When you think about it, ice cream is a highly artificial food, since snow and fully ripe fruits are seasons apart. No matter. Everybody needs a little summertime snow to cool off their mouths. The next section has some simple ice cream you can make at home.

EASY VANILLA

This is not the cranky kind of ice cream. It is the still frozen sort that comes to life in a freezer tray, and it's easy enough for a kid to make.

1. Put these things in a pot:
½ cup sugar
¼ teaspoon salt
1 cup milk
3 beaten egg yolks

2. Cook them gently. Keep stirring them until they begin to bubble.

COOK THE LIQUID. LET IT COOL.

WHIP THE CREAM

FOLD THE LIQUID INTO THE CREAM.

FREEZE IN TRAYS. STIR OFTEN THE FIRST HOUR.

3. Put the liquid in the freezer until it becomes slush.

4. Meanwhile it's time to make the cream part. Put these things in a mixing bowl:

1 cup whipping cream

1 teaspoon vanilla

Beat until the cream stands in soft peaks. If you beat it any more, you will have greasy tasting ice cream.

5. Pour the cold slush into the cream. Stir it around, trying not to smash the whipping cream.

6. Freeze this mixture in two ice cube trays until it is firm. Stir it a couple of times the first hour. It should be done in 3 to 4 hours. This recipe makes about a quart.

You can flavor this basic recipe with chocolate or spices. Add fruit, nuts, or chocolate chips toward the end of the freezing. Invent your own flavor. How about pickle ice cream?

SEND AWAY:
COLD FACTS

A cook was beheaded in 1649 by Charles I of England for divulging the secret of making ice cream or as he called it "frozen milk."

Popsicles were first called "epsicles" after their inventor, a Mr. Epperson, who discovered them by accident. He found a frozen glass of lemonade on a windowsill with a spoon in it. Being a stand man at an amusement park, he could see it had possibilities. He named it after the icicle, substituting the first letters of his name. Find out more fascinating cold facts in

a free 18 page booklet called "The History of Ice Cream." Write to:

International Association of
Ice Cream Manufacturers
910 Seventeenth St, N. W.
Washington, D. C.
20006

ICE TREATS

Frosted glass with class. Dip the rim of a glass in water or juice. Then dip it in granulated sugar. Stash it in the freezer for a few minutes. Fill it with fruit juice.

Rinky dink ice. Place slices of fruit in the bottom of a ring pan. Just cover them with water. Freeze it. When hard, add more water. Freeze it solid. Unmold it and float it in a punch bowl for a little visual delight.

FRUIT CUBES — MINT, STRAWBERRY, LEMON

RINKY-DINK ICE — FRUIT SLICES

ICE CREAM

FRUIT BOMBES

FRUIT CONCENTRATE — GINGER ALE

SLUSH

Juice cubes. Freeze fruit juice into cubes. Toss them into ginger ale for a taste treat.

Slush or can-can delight. This is a good one to make if there is a lot of leftover canned fruit syrup around your house. Save it and freeze it. One cup of broken frozen juice can be beaten or blended into a frappe. Serve with a straw.

Fruit cubes. Ice cubes with fruit. Mint, cherries, and lemon twists give a drink color. They also give you something to look forward to at the bottom of the glass.

Frozen bombes. Hollow out an orange or lemon cutting the top to make a hat. Fill with ice cream or iced fruit juice and yogurt. Put the hat back on and freeze. Thaw it for 20 minutes before eating.

FROZEN BANANAS

This recipe makes six frozen banana pops. To make them you'll need to buy:
a small package of chopped nuts
3 bananas
a 12 ounce package of chocolate chips
some wooden skewers for handles

Plus you'll need about 1½ tablespoons of vegetable oil and an empty 6-ounce frozen juice can.

1. Peel bananas, then slice them in half crosswise.

2. Stick a skewer in each banana and freeze on separate pieces of foil or waxed paper.

3. When the bananas have been in the freezer for half an hour, fill a saucepan half full of water and begin to heat it. Meanwhile fill the juice can with half the package of chocolate chips (¾ cup) plus 1½ tablespoons oil. Then put can inside of saucepan to melt chocolate.

4. Take each banana out of freezer separately and dip into the chocolate liquid. Give a banana a turn as you pull it out of the liquid. Then, if you like, roll it in nuts while it's still wet. Rewrap each banana in foil and put it back in freezer for ½ to 1 hour to finish freezing.

JUICE POPSICLES

Juice bars are a yummy cooler downer on a hot day. Make them out of limeade, orange juice, grape juice, or your favorite juice.

You will need:
paper cups
wooden skewers or sticks for handles
a small can of frozen juice concentrate

1. Mix the contents of the frozen juice can with 1½ cans of water in a jug.

2. Fill each cup about 2 inches full with this mixture, then put the cups in the freezer.

3. Check the cups in about 45 minutes. When ice crystals have begun forming in the juice, sink a skewer stick into the center of each cup.

When the popsicles are frozen, peel the cups away and eat them.

WATERMELON ICE

A wonderful light pink ice dessert.

1. 2 cups blended up watermelon. Cut up chunks and remove the seeds beforehand.

2. Chill.

3. Fold in ½ cup whipping cream for a sherbet sort of taste.

WATERMELON HEARTS

Another way to eat one of the all time best summer fruits.

Cut ¾ inch slices. Using a knife or big cookie cutter carve or press out shapes. Stick them on a skewer. Chill. Make watermelon ice with leftover sections.

SEEDS

One of the best things about eating watermelons is the seeds. Some people just spit them out. They are the unlucky ones who have never known the thrill of shooting these slick little seeds at high speeds to bull's eye your opponent.

Watermelon seed shooting is a fine art, not to be confused with the lowbrow seed spitting sometimes resorted to by the unskilled.

Watermelon seed wars are best fought in the evening about dusk. Start with a big slice of juicy watermelon. Combat can be carried on as your mouth enjoys itself. Eating is a hand-to-mouth operation. Hold the wet seeds between thumb and forefinger. Point and press. You should be able to hit a munching target at about six feet. Expect to be shot back. Watch out for sneaky shots and crossfire. Don't forget to taste the watermelon.

BUBBLES

This is a good lazy activity for hot summer days. You might notice that bubbles have longer lives on humid or rainy days. Any ideas why?

YOU CAN USE LIQUID DISH WASHING SOAP AS BUBBLE SOAP, BUT IT IS BETTER IF YOU ADD SOME GLYCERINE. BUY A SMALL BOTTLE AT A PHARMACY. POUR THE INGREDIENTS INTO A TALL THIN BOTTLE. SHAKE IT UNTIL THEY'RE MIXED.

LESS THAN ⅓ WATER

⅓ LIQUID DETERGENT

⅓ GLYCERINE

BUBBLE MACHINES

CUT A RIM FROM A PLASTIC CARTON. USE A CLOTHESPIN FOR A HANDLE.

JUICE CAN PIPE: PUNCH A HOLE IN THE TOP. CUT OUT THE BOTTOM. DIP AND BLOW.

TWIST YOUR OWN WIRE FRAMES.

STRING STRAWS

BUBBLE FRAME: FILL WITH SOAP FILM. GENTLY PULL AND SNAP.

4

GARDEN

SPRING'S SPRUNG AND SUMMER'S COME

Summertime brings sunshine, warmth, and sometimes, rain for the plant kingdom. This is all the encouragement needed to turn small seeds into a whole new world of tiny tendrils and new green leaves, blossoms, and fruits.

Take yourself outside and look around. Spring has stretched and yawned up the first leaves of the year, and now it's time for you to get out your gardening gear and start greening it up.

PLANT A GARDEN

First, you'll need a place to do your gardening. Keep these things in mind as you look for one:

1. A healthy garden must have six or more hours of sunlight each day.

2. Each plant needs water and root space to grow properly, so don't plant too close to bushes or trees.

Now that you found a good spot, collect the tools.

Tool	When To Use It
Spade/Shovel	Use it to turn garden soil.
Hoe	Use it to dig rows, hills.
Garden Rake	Use it to level garden plot, press seeds in planting. Use it to scratch away small weeds.
Scissors	Use them to thin garden plants.
Hose	For watering.
String	
	To support plants.
Garden stakes	

Now stake out the garden plot and clear away the weeds. Test to see whether the soil is dry enough to be turned. Scoop up a small handful of soil and press it gently. If it crumbles easily, it's ready to be turned. If it sticks, it's too wet. Let it dry out for a few more days.

When the soil passes the test, spade it up about 1½ feet deep and clean away any weeds or roots.

SUPER SOIL: A FORMULA

Before you do another thing in the garden, take a look at the soil there. Ideal garden soil has a loose texture and it drains quickly when it's watered. It has plenty of organic material (decayed manure and plants) and it's nearly black.

If your soil doesn't fit this description, and most don't, you can improve it by adding decayed plant material in the form of peat moss or homemade compost, and some sand. Aged manure is also a good source of organic material, but it must be aged and used sparingly.

THE GREAT PLAN

Here's a plan for a vegetable garden that measures six feet by ten feet. All the plants except for the tomato (grown from a seedling) and the green onions (grown from onion sets) are started from seed.

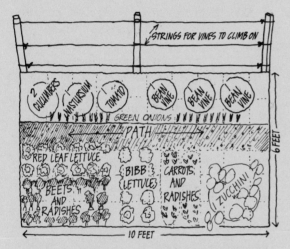

STRINGS FOR VINES TO CLIMB ON

2 CUCUMBERS · NASTURTIUM · TOMATO · BEAN VINE · BEAN VINE · BEAN VINE

GREEN ONIONS

PATH

RED LEAF LETTUCE · BIBB LETTUCE · CARROTS AND RADISHES · ZUCCHINI

BEETS AND RADISHES

6 FEET

10 FEET

THIS PLAN IS FOR A SMALL GARDEN THAT SHOULD BE A GOOD SIZE FOR A KID TO HANDLE. LAY IT OUT SO THAT THE VINES ARE PLACED AT THE NORTH PART. THIS WILL KEEP THEM FROM SHADING THE SHORTER ONES

You are probably wondering how come you need a compass to plant a garden. Your plants need to be organized so that when the sun slants in, in the morning and the afternoon, the long tall plants don't overshadow the short ones.

PLANTING DAY

Plan in hand, you're ready to get started. Begin by marking off the spaces where plants go. Use stakes and string to help mark off each area.

HOW TO READ A SEED PACKAGE

A seed package is chock full of the information you'll need to plant each kind of seed. It will tell you:
1. When to plant seeds.
2. How deep to plant each seed.
3. How far apart to plant each seed.
4. How long seeds will take to sprout or germinate.
5. How to thin out the seedlings. Hold onto your seed packages until your plants are thinned.

GARDEN KNOW-HOW

Planting in rows. Use your hoe to make a small ditch about three inches deep. Plant seeds close to one side of the row and pack earth gently over them. Water seeds by placing a slow-running hose at one end of the row.

Planting tomato seedlings. Remove seedlings from container, being careful not to disturb the soil around the roots. Deposit it in a hole a little deeper than it was in the container. Press soil firmly around the plant base leaving a basin for watering.

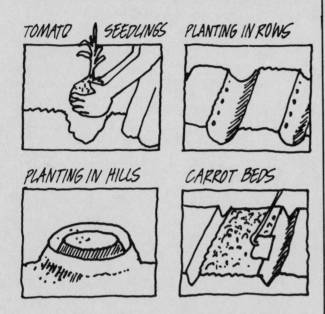

TOMATO   SEEDLINGS   PLANTING IN ROWS

PLANTING IN HILLS   CARROT BEDS

Planting in hills. Build a mound of soil a couple of inches high. Dig a wide trench around it, making its sides high enough so that when the trench is filled the seeds will get water.

Making a bed for carrots or radishes. Level out a rectangle and sprinkle seeds carefully over the whole area. Cover the seeds with soil and press the soil down with your hand or the flat part of the rake. Water carefully.

Watering. While the seeds are germinating, be extra careful when watering them so they don't wash away. Use a very slow-running hose for rows, and it's a good idea to use a watering can for extra small seeds. Planting is a little like building sand castles with moats at the beach. You have to make sure you build a garden so the water gets around the seeds and plants in the right amounts. This will take a bit of engineering.

Tomato stakes. Tomato plants need help standing up under the weight of their tomatoes. When the plants are about a foot high, drive wooden stakes in about a foot away from the stem. About six stakes will do. Encircle the stakes and plants with heavy string.

Getting advice. If you run into problems in your garden, you may need some expert advice. Ask the nurseryman or woman at your friendly local nursery. If they can't help you, you may need to take your questions to a farm advisor. Look in the phone book, under the name of the county you live in, for the Agricultural Extension Service. They also give away free booklets about growing plants and special problems.

NOW THAT
THE PLANTS ARE UP

You'll need to:

Water. Give them the watering test. Stick your finger in the soil. If the top inch of soil is dry, you will need to water them. The best time to water is in the morning or the evening. Using a hose, let the water run slowly into each row until each plant is watered. Fill basins of each individual plant.

Feed. About three weeks after the seedlings come up, begin feeding them. Buy some fish emulsion fertilizer at a nursery. Follow the package instructions and *never* use more than the instructions suggest. If you do, your plants may get sick and even die.

Thin. When seedlings are a few weeks old, you'll need to thin them. Follow the special instructions for each plant on the seed package. Use a small knife to help lift out the extra plants. Do this when the soil is damp.

Weed. Get rid of weeds, so that garden plants will have room and water to grow on. Scrape away tiny weeds with a garden tool. Pull the larger ones.

SECRET PLACE

Sometimes a person needs to get away for a while. If you don't have a special tree to climb or place to go, you can grow one. Here's how. Buy a package of seed for a vine plant such as scarlet runner beans, morning glories, sweet peas, or nasturtiums. If you have stairs or a fence, then part of your work is done. You'll also need a shovel, wood stakes, and some string.

How to Do It

1. Drive wooden stakes in the ground about three feet away from a fence or the pole.
2. Run string from the stakes to the fence or pole and tie them there.

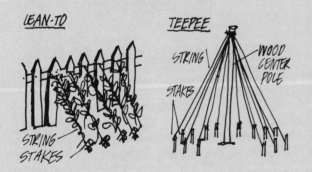

3. Plant the vine seeds according to the package instructions.
4. When the vines appear, guide them up onto the strings.

PLANT PEAS AND TRAIN THEM UP THE STRINGS.

POT GARDEN

When you don't have ground space to grow plants — all is not lost. You can grow most garden plants in containers, provided that they're big enough for the plant's roots.

You'll need:

A container. Use clay pots, plastic buckets, gallon-sized cans, etc. They must have holes for drainage in the bottom. Punch some with a nail if you need to.

Potting soil. Buy it at a nursery or dime-store.

Small rocks. Or you can use broken pieces of bricks or clay pots.

1. Put a layer of rocks in the bottom of the container.

2. Fill with soil to one inch below the container top.

3. Plant seeds in center.

WATER THE POT AFTER THE SEEDS ARE PLANTED. COVER IT WITH A PLASTIC BAG. WHEN THE SEEDS SPROUT, REMOVE THE BAG.

SUNFLOWERS

Around July, wild sunflowers begin to show their faces in fields and vacant lots everywhere. How did they get there? Perhaps a bird scattered the seed while collecting bits for a nest or its dinner. Because the wild sunflower is a native plant of certain parts of America, the seed grows easily

The sunflower's history can be traced back to certain tribes of American Indians. They cultivated sunflowers for the roots, which they roasted and ate as we eat potatoes sometimes. In the 1500s, Spanish explorers imported this

plant to Europe. You can buy these roots in the produce section of grocery stores. They are called Jerusalem artichokes.

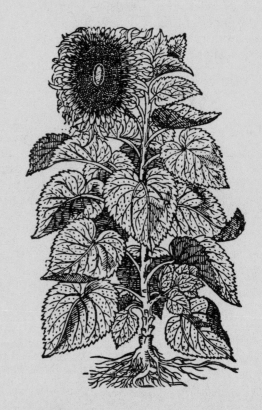

GIANT SUNFLOWERS

But what are those seeds called that come in cellophane bags? Yep, those are sunflower seeds, too. They're from a different type of sunflower though. The name is *Helianthus annuus,* the giant sunflower, and there's a good reason for the name. They can grow ten feet tall and taller.

Standing next to one will give you a bug's-eye view of the flower garden.

SUNFLOWERS TO GROW

Sunflowers are easy to grow. Choose a spot where there is sunshine all day, as sunflowers need all they can get. The soil does not have to be very rich for the flowers to grow well. Sandy soil will do.

Buy the seeds at a nursery. Plant them in a row, spacing the seeds about a foot apart and about ½-inch deep. Water them well. The seeds will take about two weeks to germinate or sprout. If you don't have ground space, you can grow them in containers, which hold at least four gallons. The soil should be made of one part pot-ting soil to one part sand. Water sunflowers whenever the soil becomes dry. Once the plants begin to form flower heads, be sure to water them a bit more often for a good crop of seeds. When the backs of the flowers turn yellowish, they are ready to be harvested. Cut them and hang them up to dry in a cool, shady place for two to three days.

MUNCH A BUNCH OF SEEDS

Remove the dried seeds from the flower heads and soak them in saltwater overnight. The next day drain them and spread them on a cookie sheet. Roast them in the oven, heated to 200 degrees, for 1½ hours or until they're crisp. You can also add some unroasted ones to your bird feeder.

P-NUTTIEST

Did you ever drink peanut milk? Wash with peanut soap? Write with peanut ink? Well, a famous American scientist by the name of George Washington Carver did. As a matter of fact, he found that he could make almost 300 different things with the peanut plant.

Peanuts, as they are called, are not really nuts. They're seed pods which belong to the pea and bean family of plants. Compare the ways a pod of green peas, a string bean, and a peanut all look. Each is a kind of fleshy envelope filled with beans or seeds.

ASK FOR FIVE-GALLON CANS AT RESTAURANTS OR ANY PLACE THAT SERVES FOOD IN BIG AMOUNTS.

Yes, the peanut is an amazing creature! One pound of peanuts contains more food value than a pound of beef steak. And that's not all. Commercial farmers plant their fields with peanuts to enrich the soil with nitrogen, a valuable plant food which most plants steal away from the soil.

PEANUT FARM

Buy some unroasted peanuts at a health food store. Remove the shell, but be careful to leave the red skin on. Soak the seed in water overnight. The next morning put the peanut on top of some yarn in a jar. Add a teaspoonful of water and check daily to keep the yarn moist. Soon the nut will grow a root. When the root three inches long, plant the peanut in an eight-inch pot. Use potting soil and pebbles for drainage. In six to eight weeks the plant will grow yellow flowers. After each flower pollinates, it will fall off. A sort of green finger called a peg will emerge and find its way back into the soil. You won't be able to see it happen, but the peg will become a peanut there. In another four to six weeks, when the green part of the plant begins to turn brown, it's time to harvest the peanuts. Take hold and pull the whole plant up. Behold! Peanuts!

A ROAST TO BOAST ABOUT

Soak your peanut harvest in salted water overnight. Spread them in one layer on a cookie sheet and roast them for three hours at 250 degrees. Then eat.

ADD PAPER EARS AND YARN HAIR.

If you're sitting around sharing them with your friends, you might like to save the shells to make peanut puppets. Draw faces on with ink markers.

PEANUT BUTTER

Make peanut butter at home with a blender. Combine the cup of roasted peanuts with two tablespoons of vegetable oil. Grind this mixture in the blender as much as you like. If the peanuts aren't salted, add ½-teaspoon salt.

SEND AWAY:

GOOBER NEWS

Want to know more about peanuts or peanut history? How about a peanut plant poster or a booklet about the famous peanut scientist George Washington Carver, or a recipe for Mississippi Mud Cake? You can get these and the answers to any peanut questions you might have from:

Peanut Food Promotions
P. O. Box 1709
Rocky Mount, North Carolina
27801

SOME PUMPKIN SEEDS

Save your pumpkin seeds for a real treat. Wash them with cold water. Spread them on a cookie sheet and roast them in an oven at 300 degrees. Turn them to toast on both sides. Salt and eat them.

CULTIVATING CALABASHES

Holy Smoke — What do you suppose it is?

Well, a calabash is a bottle gourd, and bottle gourds have been cultivated by folks in this country and others for centuries. Because of their shape, they readily become bottles, bowls, ladles, etc. In India, a musical instrument called the sitar is made from this type of gourd. In Europe, tobacco pipes are crafted from the calabash.

Like its cousins the watermelon, cucumber, cantaloupe and pumpkin, the calabash is a vining plant. It's a plant that likes to creep and crawl. In other words, it's a vine. It prefers a bit more sun though, so if you live where the summers are hot, you can expect your vine to thrive. You'll need to allow about one square foot for each plant, and see that it has a trellis or fence to climb. You might put a trellis in front of a southerly exposed window, for a living curtain and an inside view of how it grows.

Planting

Buy a package of seeds for bottle gourds (botanical name, *lagenaria*). First soak the seeds overnight. Plant them in full sun when the weather is warm, ½ inch deep and six inches apart. When they have three leaves, thin out to 12 inches apart. Feed them according to the directions on a package of all purpose plant food, from age three weeks on. After the gourds begin to form, you can do some experimenting. By binding a gourd with cloth or rope, you can mold the way it will turn out. Try etching a pattern on a gourd with a nail or pointed tool. When the gourd is ripe, the stem will dry. It is then time to pick the gourds. Clean all the soil off, and then wipe them with rubbing alcohol. This will kill any germs which might rot the gourds before they can dry. You can hang them up or put them in a box to dry. Be sure that they are not touching each other. Drying will take a couple of weeks.

Decorating Them

This method is used by African women to decorate calabashes for use in their kitchens.

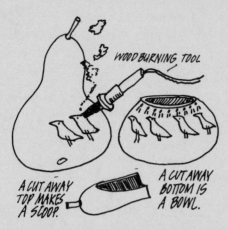

A CUT AWAY TOP MAKES A SCOOP.

A CUT AWAY BOTTOM IS A BOWL.

You'll need a package of Rit dye of a dark color. Dip your gourd in the dye until it turns the color of the dye. Rinse it once in cool water, then let it dry on some newspaper. When dry hang it in a smoky place such as a fireplace. Be careful that it doesn't get too hot and burn. Polish it from time to time with a soft cloth. The whole process will probably take several days and will produce a shiny finish.

To draw designs on gourds, you can use a woodburning tool to etch them in. You'll find that it's easier to make your designs run lengthwise on the gourd.

CALABASH CANTEEN

This is just the thing to carry water on a hike.

1. Choose a round, dry gourd. Remove the stem end with a small hand saw and scrape the inside out. Decorate or paint the gourd if you like.

2. Cut four 18-inch lengths of string. Join them on a small ring. Using square knots tie a net to fit the gourd.

3. Add loops to attach to your belt and cork to fit.

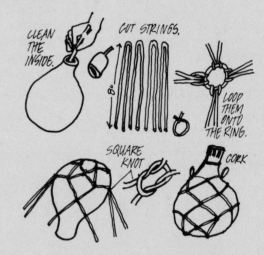

GARDEN BIRDS: THE BUG POLICE

A garden is a natural bird attraction because it offers them food, drink, and water for them to bathe in. If your garden place has trees or bushes nearby, chances are that some birds will be making themselves at home there. That might be a good thing for your garden and your bird neighbors.

Besides being interesting creatures, birds are probably the best insecticides around. Though certain kinds of birds may help themselves to an occasional bite of your garden, think about encouraging them to stay on in your garden. You can do so by adding special feeding, watering, — and for some kinds of birds — nesting places.

HOUSE A BIRD

Only a few kinds of birds will live in man-made birdhouses. Wrens, swallows, and martins — which are especially hungry bug-eaters — will be quite willing to move into such a birdhouse. Be sure that you hang them in a quiet place, out of the reach of cats.

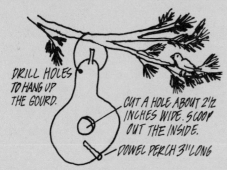

DRILL HOLES TO HANG UP THE GOURD.

CUT A HOLE ABOUT 2½ INCHES WIDE. SCOOP OUT THE INSIDE.

DOWEL PERCH 3" LONG

This is an old idea for a martin or swallow house. Some tribes of farming Indians were believed to have hung them in their gardens to keep the birds around as bug catchers.

SEND AWAY:
PURPLE MARTIN APARTMENT HOUSE

"Did you know that an adult purple martin is claimed to be capable of eating its own weight in flying insects — or more than 2,000 mosquitos a day?

"Did you also know that purple martins are almost solely dependent on man-made housing?"

Find all this and more from Johnny Horizon's Information Sheet Number 4. It will also give you instructions on how to build a house for a colony of purple martins.

Ask for number 4. It is free from:

Consumer Information Center
Pueblo, Colorado
81009

P. S. Mark "free" on the outside of your envelope.

TAKE A CLOSER LOOK

You'll find some small creatures making themselves at home in the garden. They are bugs, spiders, and insects. From a gardener's point of view, they can be divided into two groups.

1. The bugs which mainly eat other bugs or carnivores.

2. The bugs which mainly eat plants or herbivores.

THE CARNIVORES IN YOUR GARDEN

Roll out the red carpet for this spider and insect group. It will do your garden good by dining on its natural enemies, the herbivores. Learn to recognize and protect this group.

These are some of the most common bugs of the carnivorous group that you'll find in the garden:

GOOD GUYS:	WHAT THEY EAT:
LADYBUG	APHIDS, MEALY BUGS, AND OTHER SOFT-BODIED INSECTS. A SINGLE LADYBUG CAN EAT 50 APHIDS A DAY.
LACE WING	MITES AND APHIDS. IN WARM CLIMATES APHIDS WILL LIVE THROUGH THE WINTER.
PRAYING MANTID	CATERPILLARS. MANTIDS DON'T FLY BUT WAIT FOR THEIR FOOD TO FIND THEM.
GROUND BEETLE	CUTWORMS, SLUGS, AND CATERPILLARS. THEY CLIMB PLANTS TO CATCH THEIR PREY
GARDEN SPIDER	FLYING INSECTS.

BAD GUYS:	HOW TO GET RID OF THEM:
CATERPILLARS	PICK THEM OFF AND DISPOSE OF THEM.
APHIDS	FIND THEM ON THE UNDERSIDES OF LEAVES. PUT A HANDFUL OF OLD-FASHIONED LAUNDRY SOAP IN A BUCKET OF WARM WATER. DIP THE APHID-COVERED LEAVES. IT WON'T HURT THE PLANTS.
SPIDER MITES	FIND THEM ON THE UNDERSIDE OF LEAVES. SPRAY THE PLANTS WITH WATER. PICK OFF LEAVES WITH EGGS AND BURN THEM.
CUTWORMS	FIND THEM AT THE BASE OF PLANTS. MAKE COLLARS FROM MILK CARTONS TO PROTECT YOUNG PLANTS. REMOVE TOP AND BOTTOM.

BUG OFF
THE PLANT EATERS

The herbivorous group of insects is the one most gardeners would rather steer clear of. The word *herbivorous* means plant eating, and for your garden's sake, you might have to declare all out war on the little buggers.

In a small garden, the best way to beat bugs is to hunt them down and take them off with your hands. Avoid using poisons — sprays or powders — to get rid of garden pests. They will kill the helpful, carnivorous insects along with the garden eating herbivores.

SEND AWAY:
ESCARGOTS

Feeling adventurous? You can think of those pesty snails that are taking bites out of your garden as the makings of a gourmet meal. In fact, those very snails may be the descendants of the French vineyard snail which was imported into this country around 1850 as a taste treat. Snails have long been cultivated in Europe in dooryard cages for food. They are high in protein, rich in minerals, low in calories, and as the booklet says, "Tasty . . . ." Better than baloney.

If you want to know how to collect and prepare *escargots* (es CAR go) — the French and fancy way to say snails — then write for, "Snails as Food, Escargots," leaflet 2222. It is free from:

Publications
University of California
Division of Agricultural Sciences
1422 South 10th Street
Richmond, California
94804

After all, free snails — free instructions. Free your mind for a free meal.

SEND AWAY:
"PESTICIDES ARE PERILOUS"

The problem with pesticides is that they are poisonous. Once you start spreading poison around your environment, it has a way of getting into the mouth of an innocent bystander. Even though chemical companies try real hard to make poisons that are selective killers, it often doesn't work out that way.

The best solution is to use nonchemical means of getting rid of those treacherous tomato worms and obnoxious onion flies. This reprint will give you some help as well as some easy-to-read information. One copy of "Pesticides are Perilous" is free from:

Educational Servicing Station
National Wildlife Federation
1412·Sixteenth Street, N. W.
Washington, D. C.
20036

DRY IT UP

Drying is an old method of preserving fruit or vegetables. The whole idea is to take the water out of the fruit, so that water loving bacteria will not grow and spoil it. Here's what you'll need to dry fruit by a simple method:

Fruit, some cheesecloth, a clean sheet, sunshine, and a table or drying surface.

PEACHES, APRICOTS, AND NECTARINES

All of these may be dried in pretty much the same way. Wash and peel them. Remove the seeds and slice the fruit into ½ inch thick pieces. Spread these pieces on a sheet-covered table or a board outside where there's sun all day. Be sure the slices aren't touching each other. While they are drying, cover them with cheesecloth to keep the bugs off, and turn the slices when the top-side begins to dry. You may take the fruit in at night so that moisture from the night air doesn't slow down the drying process. When the fruit is dry, store it in closed containers.

APPLES

Should be peeled, with the whole core taken out, leaving a hole in the center. Slice the apples crosswise to a ½-inch thickness. The slices should be doughnut shaped.

String the rings on a pole or a broomstick and hang them to dry. Other things that you can dry are: whole berries, plums, pineapples, and even vegetables.

FRUIT LEATHER

Making fruit leather is a super way to preserve ripe fruit for a hiking snack or an anytime snack. You can make it out of your favorite fruit. Here's how:

1. Wash and take the seeds out of 4 cups of fresh fruit: nectarines, berries, peaches, plums, or apricots. Cut large fruits in half. Combine the fruit in a saucepan with ¼ cup of sugar. Heat this mixture almost to a boil (180 degrees), then crush with a potato masher.

2. Put the hot mixture in a blender and puree it or push it through a sieve. Cool it until it's lukewarm. Pour on a plastic sheet and spread to ¼ inch thickness on the drying surface.

3. Drying surface: cut a piece of plastic wrap 18 inches long and tape it down to a clean table or board that can be placed in full sun all day long. When it's dry, roll up the leather and wrap and store it in a cool, dry place.

4. How to know when it's dry: fruit leather will take a day or two to dry. When it's dry to the touch, test it by trying to pull the fruit leather away from the wrap. If it doesn't peel off in one piece, dry it longer.

SUN JAM

Berry or apricot. To make an 8-ounce jar of jam you'll need these ingredients:

1½ pounds ripe apricots or berries
1 cup of sugar
2 teaspoons lemon juice

1. Wash the fruit. Cut apricots in quarters and take out the seeds. Mix all the ingredients in a saucepan. Cover the pan and leave it at room temperature for 1 hour.

2. Put saucepan on the stove and bring the mixture to a boil. Boil for 5 minutes without stirring, then take the pan off the stove and let it cool for 30 minutes.

3. Pour the cooled mixture into a 9x9 inch baking pan and cover it with a clear plastic wrap.

Put the pan on a table outside, where it will get sun all day long. In about 3 to 8 hours, when the jam is about as thick as syrup, pour it into an 8 ounce jar. Then store it in the refrigerator.

FRUIT DETECTIVE

So you live in a city surrounded by sidewalks and blocks of buildings? The closest you come to nature is passing the Boston fern in the hall? How are you supposed to know what is ripe out there in the country?

There are ways:

Use your head for shopping. You know that when strawberries in the supermarket stop being 89 cents a basket, and suddenly drop to three for $1.00, then it is strawberry season, and a good time to make strawberry sun jam.

Get to know the fruit and vegetable man. You can ask him something like "Hey, mister fruit man, when are the peaches going to be cheap?" Produce buyers know these things. Maybe he can get you a lug of something for a little less. It never hurts to ask.

Find a pick-it-yourself farm. Taking a drive to the country for apples or pears can be a good time for everybody in your family. Sometimes these places are listed with the local Chamber of Commerce. Check the newspaper classified ads. Keep your eyes peeled when you are out cruising around.

Listen to the news. Many radio and TV stations have something called "farm report." They will give you an up-to-the-minute survey of what is ripe out there in the fields, and what is a good buy at the produce bin.

5

SUMMER BIRDS

SUMMER BIRDS

Every area has its resident birds who stick around all year long. Once it warms up, the bird population should boom because the ones who winter in warmer spots fly back to breed, maybe in your backyard. Exciting!

Summer is a good time to watch birds. In many areas April, May and June are the times when birds are looking their gaudy best in breeding plumage and singing their hearts out, trying to attract a mate. They nest in the spring and will raise their young in the summer. This whole process will be delayed in the high places where spring gets a late start. Keep your eyes and ears open to find out what your local birds are doing this summer.

BIRD FEEDERS

You are not saving a bird's life by making a wild bird feeder. What you are doing is spreading out a little incentive so that they will show themselves. Birds are fun to watch, and they can make your backyard a more interesting place. Besides it's nice to have a few friends of a different species.

When you put out a bird feeder, you are changing the ecology of the area. Your local birds can become dependent on a free meal. In the summer this isn't too dangerous. There should be plenty of other foods available in the neighborhood. In the winter, when food is scarce, forgetting to fill the feeder is disaster for your bird friends. So unless you are willing to make sure the feeder is full at all times, feed them only part of the time. This way they will treat your place as dessert rather than the main course.

On the other hand, if you want your bird friends to stick around and are sure you won't neglect them, late summer and fall are the best times to feed. This is before the birds have settled down on their wintering grounds and fixed their food hunting habits for winter. But you better not let them down.

WHERE TO PUT IT

Put the bird feeder where you can see it. After all, you're feeding the birds for your pleasure as well as theirs. The ideal spot is one where you can see the feeder from a window, but near enough to trees or shrubs so that the birds can check it out without exposing themselves too much. Ten to twenty feet from shrubs or trees is fine. Look for a spot that will give some shelter and protection from wind and rain.

Take care to find a spot that won't be vandalized by other animals. If you want to look at birds, it won't do, having squirrels eating up the seeds. Also cats have a habit of mugging bird visitors to your feeder. So place it well out of leaping distance from ledges and branches.

When first setting up your bird feeder, make sure the food is in plain view. Scatter some of it around the feeder and on the roof too, if it has one.

BIRD FEEDERS TO BUILD

You can build a bird feeding station out of materials from around the house. Here are some simple ways to do it:

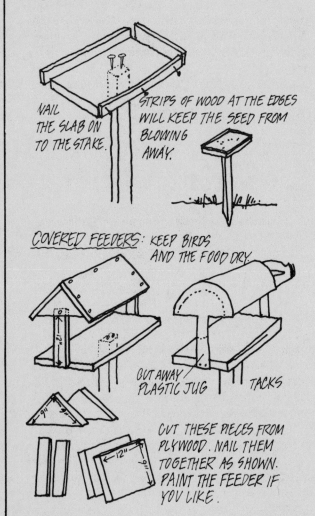

NAIL THE SLAB ON TO THE STAKE.

STRIPS OF WOOD AT THE EDGES WILL KEEP THE SEED FROM BLOWING AWAY.

COVERED FEEDERS: KEEP BIRDS AND THE FOOD DRY.

CUT AWAY PLASTIC JUG   TACKS

CUT THESE PIECES FROM PLYWOOD. NAIL THEM TOGETHER AS SHOWN. PAINT THE FEEDER IF YOU LIKE.

MILK CARTON FEEDER

USE A BIG MILK CARTON. CUT AWAY ONE SIDE

PUNCH A HOLE AND HANG IT.

WEIGHT THE BOTTOM WITH A ROCK. ADD THE SEED

PUSH A PIECE OF QUARTER-INCH DOWEL THROUGH.

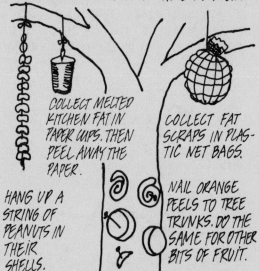

BIRD CAFETERIA: YOU DON'T NEED A FEEDER TO FEED BIRDS. HERE ARE SOME WAYS TO PUT SOME NEW ITEMS ON THE BIRD MENU.

COLLECT MELTED KITCHEN FAT IN PAPER CUPS. THEN PEEL AWAY THE PAPER.

COLLECT FAT SCRAPS IN PLASTIC NET BAGS.

HANG UP A STRING OF PEANUTS IN THEIR SHELLS.

NAIL ORANGE PEELS TO TREE TRUNKS. DO THE SAME FOR OTHER BITS OF FRUIT.

SO WHAT DO BIRDS EAT?

That depends on the birds.
Some eat fish.
Some eat plants that live on pond bottoms.
Some eat carcasses of dead or almost dead things. My advice is not to put out any animal carcasses on your bird feeder in hopes of attracting a vulture!

Stick to things like seeds or foods that your local backyard birds might find tasty. Of course you could branch out and supply some insects plucked from your garden, sugar water, or a bit of fruit to attract a wider variety of customers. Here is a list of common birds and their favorite foods.

KIND OF BIRD	FAVORITE FOODS
SPARROW, JUNCO, FINCH	SUNFLOWER SEEDS, NUTS, CORN
BLACKBIRD, CARDINAL, TOWHEE, JAY	BREAD CRUMBS, SMALL SEEDS
NUTHATCH, TITMOUSE CHICKADEE	FAT, CRUMBS, PEANUTS, SUNFLOWER SEEDS
ROBIN, MOCKINGBIRD, CAT BIRD, THRUSH	ORANGE, APPLE BITS, CRUMBS, RAISINS
HUMMING BIRD	SUGAR WATER

You can buy a supply of wild bird seed from a pet store or food market. It will go farther and cost less mixed with equal parts of chick feed. Buy chick feed from an animal feed store.

Be warned: birds don't always eat what the books say they will. So don't be surprised when you find a chickadee doing acrobatics sipping from the hummingbird feeder. Even birds break the rules.

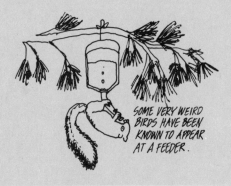

SOME VERY WEIRD BIRDS HAVE BEEN KNOWN TO APPEAR AT A FEEDER.

BIRDBATHS

Have you ever noticed how birds fly out of nowhere when the lawn sprinklers go on?

Water is as important to birds as food. In the summer in dry places, it can be more important and at least as attractive. Maybe your backyard needs a birdbath or shower. Discovering the water habits of each species of bird will take some experimenting on your part.

A birdbath should be shallow. It should have a lip for the bird to rest on. The bottom should not be slick. A ceramic or plastic container will make a good bath. Don't use metal though, because it will heat up in the summer and freeze in the winter — either sticking or scorching birds' feet. Remember to change the water often.

BIRD BATHS

EARTHEN WARE PLATE MADE FOR SITTING UNDER PLANT POTS.

GARDEN HOSE

SHALLOW PLASTIC DISH

MAKE A STAND FROM WOOD SCRAPS ..

BLUE BIRDS ESPECIALLY ENJOY A FINE SHOWER. SET UP A NOZZLE THAT MAKES A SPRAY. PUT IT WHERE YOUR WATER LOVING PLANTS WILL ENJOY IT TOO.

POUND A WOODEN STAKE INTO THE GROUND. TIE ON THE HOSE AND NOZZLE.

DOVES FEED AND DRINK IN THE EVENING LET THE WATER RUN SLOWLY IN THE GARDEN. ITS A GOOD TIME TO WATER THIRSTY PLANTS AND BIRDS.

WHO GOES THERE?

You can have a good time watching the activity at your feeder without knowing a thing about birds. Perhaps you would like to be on a first-name basis with the feathered locals. What you need is an expert. If you don't know any experts, the next best thing is a bird identification book. Your local library is sure to have one. You will be most interested in the perching-bird section.

Once you get the book open, you'll find that suddenly all birds look alike. So before you look in a book, take a good gander at the bird. Try to remember the general colors and markings.

At first it will be hard to see everything before the bird flits away. You might want to start a notebook with drawings to help you remember. Jot down information like what the bird ate and where you saw it — if it was away from the feeder. All these clues will help you discover the bird's identity.

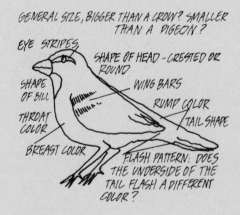

GENERAL SIZE, BIGGER THAN A CROW? SMALLER THAN A PIGEON?

EYE STRIPES

SHAPE OF HEAD - CRESTED OR ROUND

SHAPE OF BILL

WING BARS

THROAT COLOR

RUMP COLOR

TAIL SHAPE

BREAST COLOR

FLASH PATTERN: DOES THE UNDERSIDE OF THE TAIL FLASH A DIFFERENT COLOR?

AUDUBON

See a bird you can't identify? Need some advice on bird first aid? Want to go on a bird walk? Your local Audubon Society can help. Look for their number in the phone book. Most areas have a club with enthusiastic birders. "Birder" is another name for a bird nut. Auduboners are all ages.

SEND AWAY:
BIRD BOOK

Want to know more about bird watching? The National Wildlife Federation has a really nice color booklet that will help you spot and identify birds. It has a checklist of birds common to America. It's called, "Bird Watching with Roger Tory Peterson." He is a famous bird expert. Single copies are free from:

National Wildlife Federation
1412 Sixteenth Street, N. W.
Washington, D. C.
20036

SEND AWAY:
BIRD FLASH CARDS

You can get to know birds in a flash with Audubon bird cards. They are postcard size. One side has a beautiful bird in living color; the flip side has a description and other bits about the bird's life-style. They would make nifty pin-ups. They come in sets of 50. (Can you imagine all 50 flying above your bed?) Each set costs $4.20. You can choose from: Western Birds, Winter Birds, Spring Birds, Summer Birds. Write to:

Educational Services
National Audubon Society
950 Third Avenue
New York, New York
10022

P. S. Ask for their catalogue. They also have posters and other nature study stuff.

BIRDS YOU WON'T SEE AROUND YOUR FEEDER

It's very unlikely that you will see any bald eagles or turkey vultures or owls or egrets or gulls around your feeder. You might as well look for your shoes in the refrigerator. It's just the wrong habitat.

Habitat? Habitat is the place where something lives. Besides being a place, it's all the other things a creature needs to survive, like food, water or lack of it, tree cover or high grass, or rocky slopes.

Expect seed eating creatures to show up if you're serving seeds at your bird feeder.

SEND AWAY:

HABITAT POSTERS

How about a big, beautiful, hand-drawn poster to liven up your habitat? These 23 inch by 29-inch posters show animals and plants in their special communities. One is of the grasslands. The other is the freshwater pond. Both come with a guide. They are $1.85 each postage included. Order them from:

The Book Nest
Richardson Bay Wildlife Sanctuary
376 Greenwood Beach Road
Tiburon, California
94920

HUMMINGBIRDS

Hummingbirds don't hum — at least they don't hum tunes. They do make a kind of whirring noise with their fast wingbeats. They can fly up to 50 miles an hour and they can fly backwards. Pretty impressive stuff for the smallest of birds in North America. One bird book describes them as "fearless and pugnacious." What they mean is that if the hummingbird feeder is empty and you are sitting nearby, you are likely to get buzzed until you fill it up.

You will have to use special tactics to attract these winged beauties to your backyard. They have a very specialized mouth — a long thin beak for sipping flower nectar. Birdseed looks about as tasty to a hummer as an old shoe, but sugar water is a sure thing.

Here's How:

1. Dissolve one part sugar in 3 parts hot water.
2. Add a few drops red food coloring, or better yet, some red beet juice. It's probably a lot healthier for the birds. Let it cool. At first the solution needs to be bright red. Hummers are attracted to red. Later you can taper off to pale pink. (If you are ever walking along and are suddenly buzzed by a hummer, it's because you are wearing red. Those birds think you're some weird kind of walking flower.)
3. Put the solution in a feeder. Hang it near flowers, or in plain view of any passing hummers.
4. To make a homemade feeder, tie a small medicine bottle around its center with a string. Hang it from a tree.

6

INSECTS

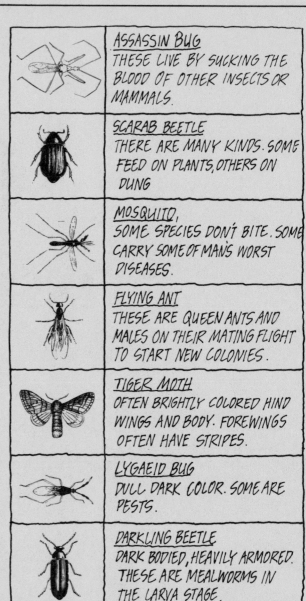	**ANT LION** THESE ARE DOODLE BUGS IN THEIR LARVA STAGE. THEY DIG PITS FOR TRAPPING ANTS.		**ASSASSIN BUG** THESE LIVE BY SUCKING THE BLOOD OF OTHER INSECTS OR MAMMALS.
	LACEWINGS PALE GREEN WITH GOLDEN EYES. GARDENERS LIKE THEM BECAUSE THEY EAT APHIDS.		**SCARAB BEETLE** THERE ARE MANY KINDS. SOME FEED ON PLANTS, OTHERS ON DUNG
	NOCTUID MOTH HEAVY-BODIED HAIRY MOTH. KNOWN AS CUTWORMS IN THEIR LARVA STAGE.		**MOSQUITO** SOME SPECIES DON'T BITE. SOME CARRY SOME OF MAN'S WORST DISEASES.
	CLICK BEETLE REDDISH BROWN. THEY ARE NAMED FOR THE NOISE THEY MAKE WHEN THEY FLIP OVER FROM THEIR BACKS.		**FLYING ANT** THESE ARE QUEEN ANTS AND MALES ON THEIR MATING FLIGHT TO START NEW COLONIES.
	SNOUT MOTH BROWN OR GREY. THEIR MOUTH PARTS STICK OUT IN FRONT OF THEIR HEADS.		**TIGER MOTH** OFTEN BRIGHTLY COLORED HIND WINGS AND BODY. FOREWINGS OFTEN HAVE STRIPES.
	CRANE FLY LIVES IN MOIST PLACES AND FEEDS ON DECAYED PLANT MATTER.		**LYGAEID BUG** DULL DARK COLOR. SOME ARE PESTS.
	TYPHIID WASP PARASITIC WASP LIVING ON BEES AND OTHER WASPS. FEMALES STING.		**DARKLING BEETLE** DARK BODIED, HEAVILY ARMORED. THESE ARE MEALWORMS IN THE LARVA STAGE.

SUMMER IS BUG TIME

Insects seem to crawl out of everywhere to flit, buzz, and be generally annoying. They seem to have nothing better to do than fly in your eyes or walk all over the pickles when you're on a picnic. That's when they aren't biting your ankles.

Bugs are not all bad. In fact, bugs, once you learn something about them, can be fascinating little fellows. They are certainly some of the most varied and successful creatures on the earth.

The best part is, that once you get acquainted with insects, their presence won't bug you half so much.

LAZY PERSON'S BUG COLLECTION

If it's summer, you probably already have the beginnings of an insect collection and you don't know it. Check around under your outside porch light. Do you see any bug bodies? No? Either you have a very efficient spider or somebody just swept your porch.

You have no doubt noticed that if you turn on a white light on a warm summer night, it is soon circled by a cloud of flying things. Yup, bugs — or more properly — insects.

Ick, you think. If you can resist the urge to flick off the light and control the other common response to squish the life out of them, this is your chance to meet some insects up close. At least some of the night flying sort.

There are two ways to go about looking. One is to buy or make a killing jar. Or if you'd rather not keep a few specimens even in the best interests of science, catch them in an ordinary clear glass jar. Observe them, then set them free when you've finished.

Entomologists, the people who find insects the most fascinating of creatures, say many more insects are likely to be killed this year by insecticides than have *ever* been caught by collectors. Anyway, there is little risk of endangering most insect species — they are an extremely hardy bunch.

KILLING JAR

You can buy a professional killing jar from a biological supply house. It will most likely have a cyanide compound in the bottom. Take care to keep it tightly corked and out of the reach of young kids. *It is poison!*

You can make your own killing jar from a wide mouth bottle, like the ones that hold olives. Vitamin jars are very good because they come with their own tight fitting corks.

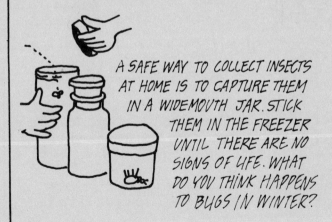

A SAFE WAY TO COLLECT INSECTS AT HOME IS TO CAPTURE THEM IN A WIDEMOUTH JAR. STICK THEM IN THE FREEZER UNTIL THERE ARE NO SIGNS OF LIFE. WHAT DO YOU THINK HAPPENS TO BUGS IN WINTER?

INSECT I.D.

You found a bug you want to keep. Or maybe you have captured something you can't name and you are curious. In the last case you should take the critter to the library and see if you can find a mug shot in one of the bug identification books. Don't put it in your pocket. You will have nothing but a handful of scales and legs by the time you arrive. This will make identification very difficult. Leave it in the killing jar or find a little box for transporting it.

No luck at the library? Check with your science teacher. If you live near an agricultural extension service, you might try there. Many states provide this information service to farmers and ranchers. Often there is a bug expert there to tell them what's chewing holes in their animals and crops.

CAPTURED BY LIGHT

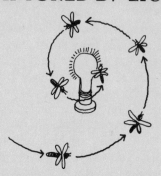

You have no doubt wondered, as you watched a cloud of kamikaze insects circling a porch light, just why these stupid bugs are trying to kill themselves.

The insects are not trying to commit suicide. They are captured by the light, which they mistake for the sun or the moon. It seems insects can't distinguish where the light comes from — they can only use it as a beacon to navigate by. The insects' navigation system worked beautifully in those ancient times when only the sun and the moon lit the earth. It has only been since humankind has infested the earth with its fires, lamps, and light bulbs, that insects have become the victims of these artificial fires.

FLYING AROUND IN CIRCLES

Away from artificial lights, the moon is the only constantly bright object in the night sky. From the viewpoint of a flying bug, the position of the moon does not change as long as the bug flies in a straight line. However, when a bug flies near a light source such as a porch light, the position of the light *does* seem to change, even when the bug is flying in a straight line.

You can see this for yourself by taking an evening stroll down a straight street. You can turn your head toward the moon at the beginning of your walk, and at the end you will still be facing the direction of the moon. But if you try to walk by a porch light, always keeping it in view, you must turn your head. The porch light is so close that its position changes relative to yours.

WALK DOWN A STREET AND THE MOON STAYS OVER THE SAME SHOULDER.

TO KEEP A LAMP LIGHT OVER THE SAME SHOULDER YOU MUST WALK IN A CIRCLE.

This change of position confuses the straight-flying bug. When the position of the porch light changes, it thinks, "Aha! I am not flying in a straight line; I'll have to make a turn to get back on course." So the bug turns toward the light to keep the light's position constant. But then the light seems to move again, and the bug thinks, "Oh-oh! Off-course again; I'd better make another turn." And the confused bug makes another turn toward the light. Finally, it reaches the light, where it becomes trapped.

INSECT ANATOMY

If you have ever crushed a beetle, you'll remember that there was an awful crunching sound. Insect skeletons are made of a substance called chitin. In a way you can say insects wear their bones on the outside.

This tough outer shell is jointed in many places, something like a medieval suit of armor. All adult insect bodies have three main segments, or parts, called the head, thorax, and abdomen. Inside these sections are the soft organs needed to keep an insect alive and kicking.

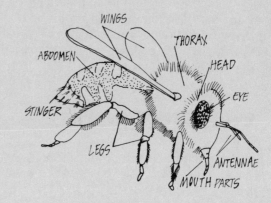

All adult insects have six legs. The easiest way to know you are looking at a true insect is to take a leg count. Also standard equipment is a pair of feelers, or antennae, and two large compound eyes. Many insects have two or three simple eyes in addition.

Some insects are winged; some have one pair, some have two pair. Some nonflying models have only stumps called the vestige wings. Some strictly ground insects have no wings at all.

Insect mouths are highly specialized according to the kind of diet. Some have chewing equipment, while others are suckers.

That sums up the basic blueprint for the insect body. Fairly straightforward, but given this basic plan there are an incredible number of variations. The Formosan Atlas moth is the size of a bird with a wing span of 12 inches. The African Goliath beetle weighs up to 2½ pounds — that's more than Kentucky fried chicken for five. Tiny wasps called fairy flies spend part of their lives inside the eggs of other insects. Other insects are remarkable for their horned plates or velvet wings or iridescent colors.

All told, there are about a million different kinds of insects. They outnumber our group of animals with backbones about 200 to 1. When it comes to body plan the insects are varied almost beyond belief.

INCREDIBLE INSECTS

Besides coming in a vast array of shapes, insects have some pretty weird habits. Did you know that:

There is a moth that sucks blood — the recently discovered vampire moth of Australia.

Some insects are poisonous — the beautiful monarch butterfly is poisonous to birds.

Some insects can raise huge blisters — the blister beetles can.

Some insects can whistle — the ghost moth whistles through its tongue.

There are insects that give presents to each other — dance flies do.

Some insects live in pools of crude oil — another talent of the amazing dance fly.

Certain insects can survive temperatures hotter than boiling water — the African midge can.

There are insects that can bore through lead shielded cables — the Bostrichid beetles are one kind of insect that the phone company could do without.

INSECT SENSE

Insects live their lives inside armor suits, a thick skin between them and the outside world. How do they keep in touch with the world outside?

Look closely and you will notice that insects are actually covered with hairs. This system of hairs attaches to nerves under the insect's skin, giving it a sense of touch. Run your finger along the hairs on your arm without touching your skin. You can feel a surprising amount. An insect can feel even more because their sensor hairs are stiff.

These hairs on the underside of a fly can not only sense touch but can also sense wind. Some scientists think these hairs are what keep a fly just out of reach of your flyswatter. As you swing what you hope is the fatal blow, these hairs sense the air movements and warn the fly of an approaching solid object, usually in time to avoid extinction. In the same way, these hairs can detect approaching solid objects while the creature is in flight. This allows it to steer clear of solid objects.

Insects are equipped with both smellers and tasters. However these chemical testing organs are not in what we would consider ordinary places. Many insects can taste something by walking on it. If it seems appetizing, a fly might make further tests with its proboscis, where the additional taste receptors are located.

Smell sensors are located in the antennae. Smell can guide an insect to food or to a mate. It can help to identify invaders from other hives or nests. You can tell smell is important to ants following a trail. You can see an ant tap its way along an ant track. Rub your finger across the trail and you will find the ant momentarily confused.

One of the most amazing feats of smell in the animal kingdom is performed by the emperor moth when finding a mate. A male emperor moth can smell the scent coming from a female moth from more than six miles away. When it does, it turns and flies upwind where the female is waiting.

BUG SENSE II

Some insects have hearing centers, usually on their legs or abdomen. These centers are the exception rather than the rule and belong to grasshoppers, moths, and locusts. Many insects like mosquitos make do with catching sound vibrations with their body hairs.

On the whole, insects are pretty quiet critters. Some, like crickets, can make a lot of noise and even have special songs for special occasions. But no insect has a set of adjustable throat strings which are necessary equipment for a true voice. However, some insects possess clever soundmakers.

Buzzes, hums, and whines are made by wing beats which vibrate the air. You know

you're safe from a humming mosquito because it can't give an in-flight bite. Watch out for the ones that are silent.

Insects' songs are provided by rubbing the rough parts of their wings or legs together. This simple action can produce a whole lot of chirps, squeaks, and creaks. It is the sound of crickets and katydids. Cicadas are able to produce a tremendous noise by vibrating a drumlike arrangement on their abdomen.

The click beetle can make a distinct click noise when it flips over from lying on its back. The deathwatch beetle makes a ticking sound as it taps its head against a hard surface.

BUG EYES

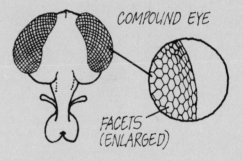

Bug eyes see differently than human eyes do. For both of us, sight is an important tool for making sense out of the world around us.

If you had the same space on your face devoted to eyes as the dragonfly does, your eyes would be the size of basketballs. But you don't need to feel cheated in the eye department. Your tiny little eyes are fine precision instruments which do a wonderful job of bringing in a fine focused picture. Fly eyes bring in a different sort of view.

A dragonfly has what are called compound eyes. Each eye is made up of many cells or facets. A dragonfly has about 20,000 facets in each eye. Facets can number less than 100 for insects with poor sight. Each facet gives an impression of dark or light. A dragonfly sees the world as a pattern of 40,000 dark and light spots. Insects can neither close their eyes nor focus.

Since many insects have eyes that extend beyond their faces, or bug out, they can see in all directions at once. Another good reason why the old flyswatter often misses its mark. Neat trick, huh?

WANT TO KNOW
HOW A BEE SEES?

Here is a little experiment you can try, to give you an idea how the world looks through an insect's eyes:

You will need a magnifying glass and a newspaper photograph.

1. Focus the magnifier on a grey part of the photo. What do you see?

2. Turn your magnifier on a corner of the TV screen — while it's on, silly. Although the TV pattern is lines rather than dots you can get an idea of how movement looks broken down into a pattern.

Of course this isn't the whole story. A bee doesn't see the same colors you do. Orange, yellow, and green all look alike to a bee, but bees can see ultraviolet — that invisible light that gives us a sunburn. So they see certain blossoms with a glow, quite invisible to us.

THEY'RE EVERYWHERE!

Once you start noticing insects you will find specimens for your studies almost anywhere. They lurk on plants, under your house, swimming around ponds, in books, happily nibbling on old clothes in trunks, scurrying around under piles of leaves, hiding out in the bark of trees.

LIKELY PLACES

Check your dog or cat for fleas, many animals have their own special kinds of resident insects.

Look in closets or boxes of papers to find wool and paper eaters.

Look under rocks (then put them back).

Take apart or slowly heat a wild mushroom to drive out the fungus eaters.

On a picnic? Leave a sandwich out in the open. Come back later to see who found it attractive.

Look around sappy trees for bees and flies.

You might set a trap by painting a section of the trunk with a mixture of molasses, sugar, and spoiled fruit juice. This is also good for moths.

Look around window sills for bug bodies.

Sift through a pile of leaves.

Pull up and look under loose bark from trees.

Check around garbage cans.

Follow your nose. Insects do. Look around flowers. Don't forget the stalks and the undersides of leaves.

Head for the bright lights. Look around store windows and street lights.

Take a grass safari. Pick a small area in a meadow or lawn. Sort through to see if anyone's there.

CAN WORMS FLY?

Strictly speaking, there is no such thing as a flying worm, at least not that we have heard of. However, if you consider that the cabbage moth flitting around your garden today was not long ago a fat, ground bound cutworm — then yes in a way, worms can fly. Except that a cutworm isn't really a worm. It's a caterpillar and a caterpillar is an insect.

Insects are surprising creatures. They live part of their lives in one body then suddenly do a quick change into a totally different form with a totally different life-style. To know what an insect looks like you might have to recognize as many as three or four separate shapes. Basically they look something like this.

Egg. All insects start as eggs. They are deposited in all sorts of places and they have all sorts of shapes, according to what kind of insect they are.

Larva. Eggs hatch into a larva or grub. These can be inchworms, furry caterpillars, or pale white maggots. Insects at this stage have huge appetites and spend all their time eating and growing. When they get too big for their skins, they molt into a new suit a size or two bigger. Larvae take big bites out of people's gardens.

Pupa. A large larva molts into a pupa. This is a resting stage that can last days or months. During this time the insect looks dead on the outside. However inside some major remodeling is going on.

Adult. The pupa splits and a totally new insect steps out. Bees, wasps, flies, butterflies all undergo metamorphosis that changes them from crawlers to winged creatures. Then the adults mate, produce eggs, and die.

Some insects don't live a life of four separate bodies. Grasshoppers, crickets, and stinkbugs skip the metamorphosis stuff. They hatch from eggs into what is called a nymph. Young insect nymphs look like their parents with some differences. They molt until they reach adult size.

THE GOOD, BAD, AND THE UGLY

Some people are quick to point out that there are many beneficial insects. What they really mean is beneficial to humans. Bees pollinate crops on which we depend for our survival. Many sorts of insects, like ladybugs and predatory wasps, feed on insects that take big bites out of our crops. Some insects have proved to be good experimental animals for scientific study. For instance, fruit flies have told us much about genetics.

We think of evil insects as ones that threaten or compete with us humans. We call them pests. (If pests are feathered or furry, they are called varmints. If they are green and growing, they are called weeds.) Some insect pests attack food plants. Aphids, scales, and caterpillars are a few of these. Even in this era of pesticides, we lose a considerable amount of our yearly crops to insects. Certain insects carry disease bacteria, like sleeping sickness which is transmitted by a fly. Malaria is spread by the bite of a mosquito.

Bubonic plague raged across Europe several times in the medieval era, wiping out vast numbers of the human population. This killer disease was spread by the bite of a flea, a terrible life-threatening pest, although people didn't know it at the time. But just suppose for a moment that the timber wolves of Europe judged the plague situation. They might have called these fleas beneficial insects, because they did such a good job of keeping the human population from encroaching on their territory — at least for a while.

It is best to remember that part of the test of a pest depends upon who is the judge.

FLY FACE

You can make an insect mask with the idea of trying to make the most realistic insect face possible. Or you can use insect mug shots to create a combination of feelers, compound eyes, and proboscises never before seen on earth. Insects masks can be used to add a little atmosphere to your room. Or you can start planning the weirdest, wildest Halloween costume to be seen in your neighborhood for many a season.

How to make your own fly face:

1. Start with a piece of cardboard. If you want to be able to wear it, make it slightly bigger than your own face. Your hand just about covers your face, so trace around it to estimate size.

2. To duplicate a real insect face, first get a good picture. Then you can either freehand it or use the mechanical method of enlarging. (The mechanical method will be explained in a minute.)

3. Cut out your mask.

4. Punch in some small eye holes. Pencil size should be fine.

5. Paint it, or color it with felt markers.

6. Punch some holes so that you can add strings for ties.

P. S. Don't be afraid to add wire antennae or glue on some fur hairs. Use your imagination.

ENLARGING

You might already know this trick for making a bigger copy of something. These directions are for enlarging an insect face, but you can do it with other things. It's a handy thing to know.

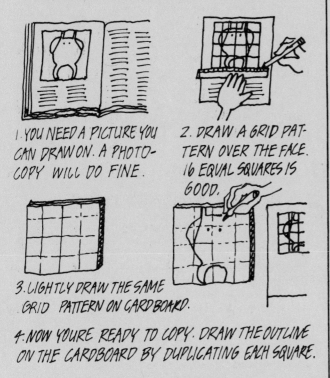

1. YOU NEED A PICTURE YOU CAN DRAW ON. A PHOTO-COPY WILL DO FINE.

2. DRAW A GRID PATTERN OVER THE FACE. 16 EQUAL SQUARES IS GOOD.

3. LIGHTLY DRAW THE SAME GRID PATTERN ON CARDBOARD.

4. NOW YOU'RE READY TO COPY. DRAW THE OUTLINE ON THE CARDBOARD BY DUPLICATING EACH SQUARE.

SEND AWAY:
AN ANT UP CLOSE

Have you ever seen an ant eye to eye? Here is your chance to look at an ant face enlarged

330 times. The Defenders of Wildlife have a free reprint called, "An Incredible, Unnoticed World." It also has some amazing pictures of a fly's lips and a wasp's back. Send a stamped self-addressed envelope to:

Defenders of Wildlife
1244 Nineteenth Street
Washington, D. C.
20036

INSECT ZOO

You might like keeping an insect around for a while for further study or just as company. People in the Orient have found crickets good company for hundreds of years. Here is a simple way to make an insect cage.

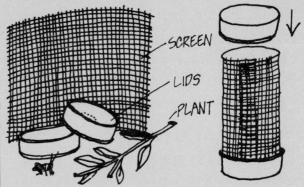

SCREEN
LIDS
PLANT

You need: Two jar lids of the same size and some wire or nylon screen. The screen needs to be smaller than the bugs you intend to keep. Window screen is good. You can get it at your local hardware store.

Here's how to assemble the cage:

1. Cut the screen about 3½ times the width of the lid's diameter. It can be any height.

2. Roll the screen into a tube shape.

3. Cap the open ends of the tube with the lid.

4. Pull off a strand of wire and secure the side.

5. Your insect cage is ready to furnish.

Now for the problem of how to furnish your insect apartment. That depends on the insect. You should try to make it as much like the captured creature's natural home as you can. Study the soil, the plants, the temperature and light, and the sort of space where you caught your insect. Try to duplicate its habitat inside your cage. One hint: when it comes to diet, vegetarians are easier to cook for than meat eaters. Omnivores, or bugs that eat both kinds of food, are easiest of all.

A good book to tell you about insect keeping is *Insects As Pets* by Paul Villard. Your library should have a copy in the kids' section.

SEND AWAY:
MEET YOUR WILD NEIGHBORS

Did you know that if you could jump as well as a grasshopper, you could leap right over your school?

Did you know that the first paper on earth was not made by people? It was made by wasps who built their homes out of it.

You can learn all of this and more from a poster called, "Bug Bits." Flip it over and the other side has a poster called, "Meet Your Wild Neighbors," which is a colorful introduction to some basic insect families. This poster comes with a four page booklet of suggestions for studying insects, a booklist, and a summer insect-watcher's chart. The booklet part is written for teachers, but the reading is easy enough for any kid who wants to be his own teacher.

For your poster send $1.25 and ask for the Insect Study Print. Mail it to:

Starting Points
520 University Avenue
Palo Alto, California   94301

SEND AWAY:
TAKE A BUTTERFLY TO LUNCH

Did you know that you can plant butterflies in your backyard? Well, you can plant their favorite foods.

The Los Angeles County Natural History Museum prints a nifty poster called, "A Planting Guide to Los Angeles Butterflies." It has great pictures. It tells what each kind likes to eat. It's mostly for the Los Angeles area but it will probably work for other places too. Send to:

The Natural History Museum Bookshop
900 Exposition Boulevard
Los Angeles, California   90007

7
CITY NATURALIST

NATURALISTS ARE ...

Many people think of naturalists as weird people who wander off to the forest to collect slimy specimens, wearing sturdy shoes, carrying knapsacks full of nature books, eating nothing but roots and berries along the way.

Not all naturalists fit this description. In fact, *you* could be a naturalist. Besides knowing the names of trees, a naturalist knows when the chestnuts are ready to roast. And where the good whistle-making trees are. And how to sneak up on a wild animal — of course it might be nothing wilder than a squirrel in the local park. And if any good pot-making clay can be found around the house. Where's the best climbing tree and the most secret spot. And how to rescue a baby bird. There are a lot of good reasons for being a naturalist.

But you can't be a naturalist? You live in the city? Horse feathers!

Lots of people think that the natural world stops at the city limits. Not true! Cities are still subject to all the natural forces that act on the country. They get rained on. Gravity still pulls down old buildings and dead trees. Water still gathers into streams and runs downhill. Stones, weather, and trees fall victim to insects and disease. Birds nest. Flowers bloom. There is a fierce competition for food and space among both people and animals.

In some ways it's easier noticing plants and animals in the city, because there are fewer of them competing for your attention. On the other hand, you might have difficulty following a creek when it disappears into a drain. Being a big city naturalist can be a little tough at times. Once you start, you'll find that the city is an exceptional place in many ways. But no real naturalist stops at the city gates.

SEND AWAY:

CURIOUS NATURALIST

The Curious Naturalist is a little magazine for young people published by the Massachusetts Audubon Society. Each issue has a theme like geography and survival, energy from waste, or how animals live together. It's good reading for beginning naturalists. It costs $3.50 for nine issues. Write to:

Curious Naturalist
Massachusetts Audubon Society
Lincoln, Massachusetts
01773

CITY SPECIALS

Natural history museums can be good places to learn about nature. You can see things in a museum that would take years to spot in the wild. And the case won't budge an inch when you press your nose up against it.

A lot of museums have special programs and films for kids in the summer. Museum bookshops are good places to buy prisms, star charts, and books on butterflies.

Museums are good places to go if you're a country kid visiting the city. See if you can talk your mom and dad into squeezing in a visit. You never see everything the first time. City kids can always go back for a visit.

Besides museums, there are a number of other spots a city naturalist might find interesting.

Zoos and aquariums: Look for collections of exotic animals. At the zoo, call ahead to find out what time they feed the lions or what they feed the snakes. Aquariums are great places to spend a hot day watching the fish floating around in their tanks.

Botanical gardens: These are plant collections. For a lot of kids botanical gardens can be dull. After all you can't watch the succulents swing around their cages or feed the ferns. What you can do is see different habitats. Visit the orchid house and see how you like steaming jungle weather. Then dash over to the cactus department and feel the desert. Stroll through a rain forest. If you are a kid visitor, botanical gardens are best in small doses. Oh yes, don't miss the weird meat-eating plants.

Arboretums: These are collections of the big woody plants called trees. No climbing allowed. Take in even smaller doses than botanical gardens.

Preserves, reserves, sanctuaries: Your city might have set aside a special wild place. It might be the address of special animals like egrets, or the site of some rare pigmy plants. Or it might be a swatch of land that has just been kept wild. Check it out, it might be worth a visit.

SEND AWAY:

NATURE NOTES FOR CITY FOLKS

The National Wildlife Federation has a set of nine sheets. The ones called "Birds of the City," "Things to Know About Bird Watching," "The Tree Squirrels," and "Creep Up On Nature" should be helpful for city nature lovers. As a bonus there are fact sheets on five endangered animals: the whales, the polar bear, the bald eagle, the American alligator, and the California condor. You can get a free set of nature notes by writing to:

Inquiry Services
National Wildlife Federation
1412 Sixteenth Street
Washington, D. C.
20036

WILD
IN THE CITY

Dubious about finding any wild animals in your city? They are out there. Seeing them may be difficult, but after all, many of them survive in the city by not being seen. Here is a list of wild beasts sometimes seen in the city. You won't find every one in your city, but who knows, you might see something not on this list. Wouldn't that be wild?

House Mouse — The common house mouse was brought to America as a stowaway. It likes dry, warm places. Success due to sharp senses, ability to reproduce well.

Norway Rat — Lives in warehouses, sewers, tunnels, Notorious carriers of disease.

Muskrats — Wild muskrats live in New York City in Cortlandt Park. And a colony has been reported on the Bronx River.

Red Fox — Foxes sometimes live on the edges of cities where there is a lot of cover. One fox was known to live under the stands at Yankee Stadium.

Bats — Nocturnal creatures found in caves or attics. Flies at night catching insects in its mouth.

Skunks — Likes all kinds of habitats. They feed at night and can be found with your nose alone.

Raccoon — Found on the outskirts of cities. Raccoons are nocturnal. They can be heard raiding garbage cans at night.

Coyote — Especially in the west. However, they have been seen in Cincinnati, Detroit, and Albany.

Squirrels Both grey and flying kinds. Red squirrels don't like cities.

Armadillo — Seem to be migrating from Central Texas. These armored critters have been seen as far north as Tennessee.

Feral Cats — These are pets or sons and daughters of pets, wild in the city.

Feral Dogs — Like cats, these wild dogs scrounge what food they can find, mostly at night. It has been estimated that 15,000 feral or wild kittens and pups are born every hour.

Birds — Many kinds (the most common are pigeons, robins, sparrows, starlings, gulls.

Insects — Of all sorts. Especially flies, fleas, roaches, sometimes butterflies.

Plus spiders, centipedes, millipedes, fish, turtles, and an occasional snake.

If you can't see animals, you can certainly see where they have been. To the practiced eye there are signs everywhere.

Read through these signs to get an idea of the sorts of clues animals leave behind. You should be able to find some animals' signs even in the middle of busy cities. Once you get started, you will be able to figure out who is around. Add your own findings to the list. Eventually you might get a reputation as the Sherlock of city park.

SNEAKING UP ON ANIMALS

Most people see very few wild animals. They don't realize how much commotion they make just walking along. To see wild animals you have to be sneaky. Here are some things to remember that will help you in getting closer to wild animals.

Try to blend into the background. Dress in colors similar to the environment. Leave your red down jacket at home, and wear various shades of one color. This will help break up your shape and make you harder to see.

Move like a cat. Make the least noise you can. Avoid crashing into the undergrowth as you move by. Move slowly and steadily with no sharp motions. Animals freeze when they sense danger. This lets them blend into the background while they figure out what is going on. You can use this trick, too.

Don't let your scent get there before you do. Approach an animal with the wind in your face, so that your smell is carried away from the animal.

ANIMAL SIGNS

Chewings and gnawings: Look under trees for chewed-on pinecones and nuts. Squirrels and birds can create quite a mess.

Nuts: Look for nuts a long way from a nut tree. Nuts are not made to travel. So they must have been carried. Jays, for instance, stash nuts a distance from the producing tree.

TRACKS: THESE DRAWINGS ARE NOT TO SCALE.

SKUNK
RACOON
COYOTE
RABBIT
PIGEON
DEER

DROPPINGS:
COYOTE
RACOON
RABBIT
SKUNK
DEER

CHEWINGS:

Tracks: These are a sure sign. The best impressions are in soft, muddy earth or sandy places. An experienced animal tracker can read a lot of information from some prints — like how old the prints are and the speed that the animal was traveling.

Scats: (droppings)

Feathers: A single feather was probably shed by a bird. A pile of feathers and bones means the bird was lunch for something else. The same goes for fur and bones. Any signs to let you know who dines here?

Trimmed trees, nibbled tips: Small trees showing no lower branches means deer munched them, especially if many trees have their lower limbs neatly trimmed to the same height.

ANIMAL WATCHING

There are a number of ways to learn about something. You can ask somebody, or you can find a book about it, or you can find out for yourself.

One of the best ways to find out about the natural world is to find out for yourself. This will save you the trouble of finding an expert or having to talk to a cranky librarian who makes it plain that anybody who cares about centipedes is crazy. Besides, it's fun to poke around outside, and a peanut butter sandwich always tastes a lot better after a few hours out-of-doors.

No muskrats? No bats? No local squirrels? And you live on the 15th floor of an apartment building, higher in the sky than most birds? Then you must turn your attention to a local animal. How about a dog? Surely there is a nearby dog to watch.

Oh geez, how boring. Before you flip the page, reconsider. Have you ever really thought about dogs? (Buying flea collars and patting them on the back doesn't count.) Have you ever thought about how a dog makes a living? Or how big its territory is? Or how weird it is that a big furry mammal with a lot of sharp meat-eating teeth cowers when you raise your voice? No? If not, you haven't started thinking like a naturalist yet.

Dogs are well-equipped hunters. They have the senses, teeth, and speed to track down and kill all sorts of smaller creatures. Coyotes, wolves, dingos are all wild cousins of our domestic dog which live quite well without any human help.

Still, the vast majority of dogs in the world make their living by pleasing people. Some are used for their tracking or guarding talents. But most of them are kept for their good looks and personalities.

Dogs are very good at pleasing people. Consider that this predator needs a big territory in the wild. An area like New York City could hold 2,500 wild dogs, at the most. Ten years ago there were more than half a million dogs in New York City. The evidence of their success litters the sidewalks and sometimes sticks to the bottom of your shoes.

CREATURE FEATURES

These are the kind of questions a naturalist might ask about a dog to get an idea of how it fits into the ecology or scheme of things. You have probably been watching dogs for years, so the answers should be easy. If you haven't, look again. You can use these questions to find out more about any critter.

How does the animal make its living? Who or what does it eat? Who eats it? How does it capture its food?

What sort of sounds does it make? What do they mean? What is its fright distance? How close can you get?

How big is its territory? How far does it travel? How wide is its range? Do you know if it lives in another state?

Does it live alone? Or is it social, living in herds, flocks, or troops?

When does it mate? Does it have any unusual mating dance like puffing out its throat, or strutting around, or diving in the air? How many young? How often? Does it shed or molt?

ANIMAL BEHAVIOR

How well do you understand dog language? Many animals have ways of communicating. Here are some things you have probably seen dogs do. All of them have meaning. How much do you understand? Turn the page for the answers.

1. WAGGING TAIL

2. NOSING AROUND

3. TONGUE OUT

4. EARS BACK, TEETH BARED

5. TAIL BETWEEN LEGS

6. HEAD DOWN, REAR UP

7. HAIR UP ON THE BACK OF THE NECK

8. EARS UP

9. LYING ON BACK, LEGS UP

10. LEG UP

DOG LANGUAGE ANSWERS:

1. HAPPY   2. NOSE TEST TO FIND IF A FELLOW DOG IS A MALE OR FEMALE. 3. A HOT DOG, DOGS COOL OFF BY PANTING 4. WARNING, KEEP YOUR DISTANCE. 5. FEAR OR SHAME 6. PLAY SIGNAL 7. READY TO FIGHT 8. ALERT. 9. SUBMISSION 10. NO THE DOG IS NOT URINATING. IT IS MARKING ITS TERRITORY WITH SPECIAL FLUID.

SEND AWAY:
RANGER RICK

Ranger Rick is a raccoon in a ranger hat. He has a lot of friends who have adventures. If you are not wild about the idea of a raccoon hero you might still like Ranger Rick's nature magazine. It is written for kids and it has great color pictures of animals like flying squirrels, jackass penguins, pork fish, and puffins. Plus there are poems, puzzles, and stories. It costs $7.00 for 10 issues. Your money also gets you membership in Ranger Rick's Nature Club. Write:

Ranger Rick
National Wildlife Federation
1412 16th Street, N. W.
Washington, D. C.
20036

NATIONAL GEOGRAPHIC WORLD

If you like looking at National Geographic, you will like National Geographic World. It is a magazine especially for kids written by the same people. It has the same super color photos and stories about wildlife and places plus stuff like sports, hobbies, and science. Then there are the puzzles, supersize pictures, and iron-ons. It costs $5.85 per year. Order it from:

National Geographic Society
P. O. Box 2118
Washington, D. C.
20013

LIFE IN THE WILD

The more of us, the less of them.

It's true of coyotes, cougars, eagles, prairie dogs, and cheetahs. The sad fact is that you don't have to shoot an animal to kill it. Just crowding these creatures into smaller and smaller corners of the earth is quite enough. We are land-improving these animals to death. Unless some plans are made, a lot of these animals will be crowded into extinction.

Most of us never notice. How can you care about coyotes if you live in the city? There are ways.

One way is to find out more about these animals. And then you can tell other people about the problems. Another way is to help the organizations who help animals. You can do this with your letters. And you can do it by joining up and supporting these groups.

Come to think of it, what a perfect place to donate the profits from a vacant lot amusement park.

DEFENDERS OF WILDLIFE

You can get a fact sheet on wolves and coyotes. They also have a good reprint about the puma from their magazine, "Defenders of Wildlife News." A student subscription costs $5.00 per year. Information is free from:

Defenders of Wildlife
1244 Nineteenth St., N. W.
Washington, D. C.
20036

WILDLIFE INFORMATION

The Sierra Club has a wildlife packet they will send you with information about whales, pumas, and wolves along with an endangered species fact sheet. They ask for a dollar donation with each packet. Also, if you have any special questions about wildlife, write to Information Services. They will do their best to answer them.

Sierra Club
530 Bush Street
San Francisco, California
94108

SEND AWAY:
PROJECT JONAH

Did you know that a Volkswagen is the same size as the tongue of a blue whale? Project Jonah will send you a kit for teachers and students with a big poster to prove it. The kit also has a book of stories and activities to tell you more about whales and what you can do to help them. Whales deserve better treatment than being made into machine oil and pet food. Don't you agree? Write:

Project Jonah
Box 476
Bolinas, California
94924

SUMMER CITY TREASURE HUNT

Once you start looking, nature crops up all over the city. Have a scavenger hunt to find difficult-but-possible natural objects in your town.

First divide your players into teams. Draw up some boundaries, maybe one city block or perhaps bigger. Then set a time limit. An hour should be enough. The teams all get a copy of the list. The time is checked and everybody rushes out to round up the stuff. The team back the soonest with the most objects wins. You will need a judge to make up the list and decide on what is fair. Your list might include:

three different kinds of grasses
a berry
a pure white rock
a sow bug
a seed pod
some natural castoff (leaves, snake skins, feathers, seeds count)
something orange
something weathered
worm food
something symmetrical
something that floats
a curly hair
a feather
the address of the animal shelter
the name of the world's oldest living thing. Hint: it's not an animal.
something wild you can eat
a thing made from oil
tracks — bring back the location
a natural freak — a four leaf clover
an example of a food producer
an egg
a leaf-rubbing

8
SLEEP OUT

BED ROLL

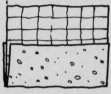

1. START WITH TWO BLANKETS.

2. LENGTHWISE FOLD ONE AROUND THE OTHER.

3. FOLD DOWN THE FLAP.

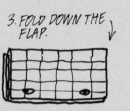

4. PIN IT WITH SAFETY PINS.

5. ROLL UP ONE END. PIN IT IN PLACE.

TENT

START WITH AN OLD BLANKET OR A SQUARE OF CANVAS.

FACE OPENING AWAY FROM WIND

STAKES. CUT SOME STURDY LENGTHS OF BRANCHES. WHITTLE THE ENDS. ATTACH THEM:

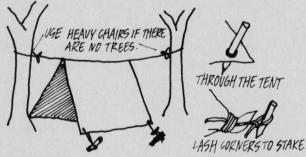

USE HEAVY CHAIRS IF THERE ARE NO TREES.

THROUGH THE TENT

LASH CORNERS TO STAKE.

PADS

FOAM PAD

COT MATTRESS

AIR MATTRESS

IF YOU ARE SLEEPING ON A HARD SURFACE, YOU WILL NEED SOME PADDING. IF YOU SLEEP ON THE GROUND, PAT THE SPOT TO AVOID LUMPS. YOU MIGHT CONSIDER DIGGING HOLLOWS FOR YOUR SHOULDERS AND HIPS.

DON'T FORGET

FLASHLIGHT

INSECT REPELLENT

SOMETHING TO DRINK

SNACKS

RADIO

SLEEPING OUT

The night turns your local environment into a whole different place. There are different smells, different insects, and different sounds, not to mention the stars. Summer is the perfect time to go out and get acquainted with the night. One of the best ways to do this is to make a bed outside and sleep out.

You don't have to go on a camping trip to sleep out. A spot in your backyard will do fine. Or, if you haven't got a backyard, try the deck or terrace or roof of your apartment building. Any place where it's flat and away from lights, if you expect to do some stargazing. Get a friend, get permission, gather up your gear, go out, and meet the night.

P. S. No matter how fearless you are, it's a good idea to bring a friend along on your sleep-out adventure. It's a good idea to have a friend along for moral support when you are trying something new. It can be one of the four-legged, furry sort, so long as it doesn't have fleas.

HIT THE SACK

The best part about summer is that you can sleep outside without much in the way of shelter. All you really need to do is find a comfortable spot, drag out your sleeping bag, and settle down for the night. If you don't have one, there is a recipe for a bed roll you can make from blankets. There are also ideas for simple shelters you can make, if you like the idea of a tent.

Who knows, you might like it outside so much you won't come in till fall.

A FIRE TO COOK ON

The best fire for a beginning backyard camper is one made from charcoal. It is a hot, fast, fairly safe fire that your local fire department won't object to. If you have an outside balcony, you can even have a cookout in a city apartment.

First get permission for a cookout from your parents. Then let them know you will need some charcoal and a can of charcoal-lighter fluid. You can buy both of these at your local supermarket. Don't forget the matches.

When you get home, you'll need to find a place to build your fire. Maybe you already have a grill or hibachi at home. If you don't, here are some ideas.

HIBACHI

IF YOU HAVE NEVER MADE A FIRE BEFORE, GET ADULT HELP.

PILED UP CHARCOALS SOAKED WITH LIGHTER FLUID.

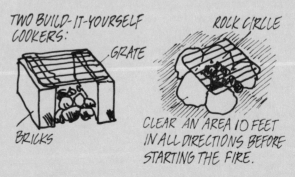

TWO BUILD-IT-YOURSELF COOKERS:

GRATE

BRICKS

ROCK CIRCLE

CLEAR AN AREA 10 FEET IN ALL DIRECTIONS BEFORE STARTING THE FIRE.

To light the fire:

1. Pile up the charcoal into a sort of a pyramid.

2. Pour on some lighter fluid. A half dozen healthy squeezes should be enough.

3. Let the fluid soak in. Meanwhile put the fluid away. You don't want it sitting around near flames, because a can of lighter fluid is a potential bomb.

4. Light the charcoal. You might want to use a long match or a tightly rolled sheet of paper so you can keep some distance. The lighter fluid will burst into furious flames.

5. The fire should be ready to cook on in about 15 minutes.

DINNER ON A STICK

There is no end to the things you can cook on a stick. Of course there is the trusty old hot dog, but did you ever consider wrapping it in a slice of bacon for a tasty change? You can use either a hand-held stick or use lots of smaller wooden sticks and lay them on a grill. You can cook sticks full of just one thing and take them away when they are done. Or you can string along a whole mix of things and cook them together for a more blended flavor.

kabobs
meat loaf
hot dogs
frozen corn
eggs and bacon
brown and serve rolls
zucchini
bread-on-a-stick

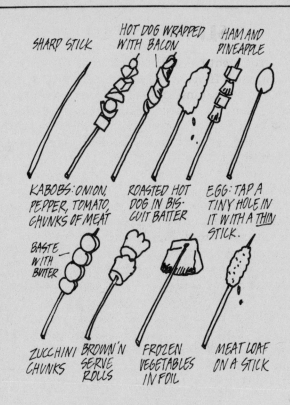

SHARP STICK

HOT DOG WRAPPED WITH BACON

HAM AND PINEAPPLE

KABOBS: ONION, PEPPER, TOMATO, CHUNKS OF MEAT

BASTE WITH BUTTER

ROASTED HOT DOG IN BISCUIT BATTER

EGG: TAP A TINY HOLE IN IT WITH A THIN STICK.

ZUCCHINI CHUNKS

BROWN 'N SERVE ROLLS

FROZEN VEGETABLES IN FOIL

MEAT LOAF ON A STICK

TIN CAN STEW

Easy to do, but you will need a hot fire for at least 30 minutes.

For each person you will need:

¼ - ½ pound ground beef
1 potato
1 carrot
¼ cup ketchup

As much onion as you think you will like (in some cases none).

Also some thick pot holders and a wooden spoon and a big 2 - 3 pound empty coffee can.

1. Set the can on the coals. Drop the meat in, to brown. Give it a stir now and again to keep it from scorching.

2. While that's cooking, slice the carrots and the onions into *thin* slices. Cut the potatoes into *little* chunks. Making small pieces hurries up the cooking, so you don't have to stand around hungry for so long.

3. Pour the cut vegetables on top of the meat. Add the ketchup. Fill the tin with enough water to almost cover everything. Don't forget the salt and pepper.

4. Fix up some sort of metal lid. Cook until everything seems done enough to eat. It should be around 30 minutes.

For gourmet tin can stew you can use your own additions like mushrooms, some bay leaves or herbs, or maybe a few spoonfuls of instant onion soup. Use your imagination.

PIG IN A POKE

Scrub a smallish potato. Core it with a knife. Stick in a sausage — smoky links are good. Wrap this creation in aluminum foil. Bake in hot coals for about 20 minutes.

ROAST CORN

This is a great way to eat corn-on-the-cob. It has a nutty flavor that will make you forget boiled corn forever. Put the corn on a grill over hot coals or push the corn ears onto sticks and hold them over the fire. Turn the ears often while they roast. Baste them with butter along the way if you like. They should be done in 15 to 20 minutes. For plumper, juicier corn, soak the ears in salt water for about an hour before roasting.

BISCUIT CUP

Scoop out the inside of a brown and serve biscuit, leaving a thick wall. Toast it over the fire on a stick, then fill it with tin-can stew.

STUFFED APPLE

Core an apple. Put brown sugar and some cinnamon in the hole and wrap it in foil and put it directly on the coals. Bake for about 30 minutes.

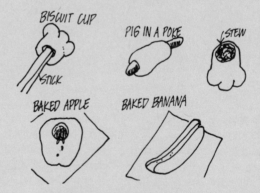

BAKED BANANA

Peel a banana. Slice it lengthwise and spread one half with honey or fruit preserves or put in a square of chocolate. Put the halves together again and cover with foil. Stick it on coals for 10 minutes.

NIGHTTIME NOISES

One of the first things you notice outside at night is how many noises there are. There are a lot of noises that are special to the night. Even the normal everyday noises seem a lot louder. There are probably a couple of reasons for this.

One is that since you can't see a lot, most of your attention has shifted over to the sound department. You notice sounds that you normally wouldn't. Also it has been shown that the human sense of hearing is more acute at night.

Besides that, sounds just seem louder at night. (No, it's not your imagination.) Sound does travel farther at night. The reason has to do with the fact that sound travels longer distances in denser materials. It's the old ear-to-the-ground effect you see in the cowboy movies. As the sun goes down, the air gets more humid. This happens because evaporating water is not dried so rapidly. As the night progresses, the air gets damper and denser. So sounds naturally travel farther in this thicker air.

If you're sleeping out in the city, the background noise level drops. Cities have a habit of humming to themselves. All the clanks, bangs, crashes, screeches, car noises, and machinery blends together to a noisy hum that tends to mask all but the loudest shrieks and sirens. So at night you tend to hear more single noises than you do in the day.

The night outside your house will have a whole set of its own special noises. Depending on where you live, you might hear the sounds of people coming and going from the local all-night grocery store. Or the sound of wind rustling through the pines. Or tree frogs. Every habitat has its own noises.

A GOOD NIGHT'S SLEEP

There are few creatures in the animal world who nod off for an all night snooze. The rhinoceros is one. However, the rhino has no natural enemies in the wilds.

So if you choose Fido as a bunk mate, don't be surprised if he jumps up a couple of dozen times during the night to sniff the air and maybe bark at the moon. Fido is no fool. Your dog's sleep pattern is naturally adjusted to survive a lifetime of outside nights.

DIDN'T SLEEP A WINK?

Many people get up in the morning insisting they didn't sleep a wink. Unlikely. What they probably mean is that it took them a long time to fall asleep and that they woke many times. Even though they slept during the night, they tend to remember the awake parts.

The human sleep pattern has several stages. Sleeping out is a good time to observe how you sleep. You will probably sleep lighter in a new environment. Your sleep pattern will be more noticeable.

The first sleep stage is the part where you feel drowsy. Gradually your muscles relax. A lot of people don't recognize this as a sleep stage. They tend to think of it more like sitting in the station, waiting to get on the bus, when in fact, the journey has begun. The drowsy stage can last a few moments or a very long time, especially if you are excited about something like leaving on vacation tomorrow.

The second stage is called light sleep. This is the drowsy half-dream state. It's the I-was-almost-asleep-until-you-came-in-and-slammed-the-door-state. Such sleepers are easily awakened and often go through some jerky motions in this stage.

The third stage is sound sleep. You can always tell when your tent partner gets to this stage; the breathing slows to an even in-out pattern. Also the muscles become very relaxed and it is very hard to be awakened.

The fourth stage or deep sleep is also called dream sleep. This is a roller coaster sleep stage. A person alternates periods of deep sleep with dreams for the rest of the night. You can tell when another person is dreaming by looking at the eyelids. Dreams are accompanied by something called "rapid eye motions." The eyes jerk around under the closed eyelids. Dreams usually happen four or five times a night sandwiched in by periods of deep sleep. The early dreams are often bits and pieces of things that happened to you during the day. The late show is often more fantasy.

Sleep is an active process, more like a journey than a single state. So when people tell you they slept like a log, you can put them straight.

Animals who are less subject to attack have long sleep cycles like our own:

ANIMAL	SLEEP PERIOD
GOATS	DOZE
ANTELOPE	DOZE
CHIMPANZEES	LONG PERIOD
MOLES	LONG PERIOD
CATS	LONG PERIOD

ON BEING AFRAID

You might not actually sleep a whole lot, at least on your first time out. All those weird noises are enough to make anybody a little nervous. And probably you spent a lot of time thinking about the possibility of getting mugged by a bear. Or maybe you were awake working out a defense plan in case a burglar should try to make off with your stash of peanut butter sandwiches. Then your mind went on to figure the possibilities of encountering a sidewinder in Cincinnati. Well, you know, the list is endless.

No, you're not crazy. Everybody is a little scared of the dark or the unknown thing lurking out there, just waiting to get you. Well whatever is out there is probably not half as horrible as the things you are imagining. Everybody is a little afraid. The trick is not to be afraid of being afraid.

Actually you should be glad about being afraid. It's your body's way of getting ready for an emergency. Your muscles become tense, ready to react in a split second. Your blood circulates faster, your breath comes faster, you are more alert and ready for any emergency.

Back in the days before locks, strong walls, and alarm systems, an uninterrupted night's sleep was a rare thing. Being a bit nervous at night was plain survival.

SUMMER SKY

Sleeping outside snuggled in your sleeping bag is the perfect opportunity to study the heavens. Any time is fine, but the best conditions are moonless or skinny-moon nights, as far away from lights as you can find. Deep, dark, country nights are perfect. The basic trick is to avoid lights which dilute the darkness of the sky and make the stars seem less bright.

Coming up is some star stuff you can try while camping out in your backyard.

HEAVENS BELOW

Tonight many stargazers will go out and look *up* at the sky. They say this even though they know perfectly well that the heavens are all around us here on earth.

The habit of saying "the stars above" got stuck in our language before we knew we were small creatures, clinging to the surface of a dirt ball, wheeling through space. In spite of what we know to be true, a lot of us have a hard time thinking of the stars as anything but above. Here is an exercise for all you secret flat-earthers.

O.K. You're outside on your back looking starward. Comfortable?

Remember you are lying on the surface of the earth. (Feel the curve in your back?) Like on some fun zone ride, you are spinning around in space. You stick to the surface because of gravity.

O. K. Now imagine that you are looking down into space rather than up at the stars. Nothing but gravity holds you in place.

Pretty scary, isn't it?

AS THE WORLD TURNS

Every night the stars wheel around overhead, rising and setting just like the sun. Unless you are already an experienced star watcher, you have probably never seen much star motion.

Here is a little trick for watching the heavens wheel round:

1. Lie flat on your back or with your head resting on the back of a chair.

2. Pick out a bright star towards the top of the heavens.

3. Line it up next to a non-moving object like a tree or a telephone pole. Fix it in your

vision so that it is just to the left of the object when you are facing south. In fact, it should be so close that it disappears when you shut your left eye.

4. Now hold your head perfectly still while staring at the star. In a short while it will disappear. You have just seen the earth move. Amazing, isn't it? At first you might not believe it. You'll think you budged or you imagined it. Try it a couple of times till you convince yourself you are riding around the sky on a ball.

SEND AWAY:
ALL ABOUT METEORITES

Did you know that meteors begin to flare about 90 miles above the earth? That the ratio of meteor body to its light trail is something like a football compared to a football stadium? Also that meteorites (the remains of shooting stars that make it to earth) are wanted for study and addition to the national collection.

You can find out almost everything you ever wanted to know about the meteorites from a booklet called "Meteorites," published by the Smithsonian Astrophysical Observatory. You can get this 18 page booklet while the supply lasts by writing to:

Smithsonian Astrophysical Observatory
60 Garden Street
Cambridge, Massachusetts
02138

MORNING DAMP

When you wake up in the morning and your sleeping bag is damp, you wonder if it rained last night. You feel the ground and it's damp too. "How could I have slept through rain?" you think. You look at your other stuff and it's damp too. "It must have rained."

Nope. Chances are you weren't rained on last night. You were *condensed* on. As the air temperature drops during the night, the air is not able to hold much water vapor. The water changes from vapor to tiny droplets. We say they condense. These droplets are pulled out of the air by gravity and land all over your sleeping self and whatever else is covering the ground. The little drops of water that collect on grass are called dew.

FIRST LIGHT

The people of Dahomey in Africa believe evil spirits that haunt the night are banished in the day. The first moment of light in the morning, not the sun, is believed to be a god.

9

SUMMER SURVIVAL KIT

SUMMER SURVIVAL

Summer is that free and easy outdoors time when you can go barefoot, wear shorts, and ride bikes. It's also the time of year when you step on bees, get sunburned, and skin your knees. Even the most cautious, fraidy-cat kids get into scrapes now and again — any kid worth his salt should know what to do with a skinned knee or a spider bite. That is simple survival, summertime — anytime.

HEAT EXHAUSTION

Heat exhaustion does not just happen to people lost in the desert. It often happens to football players practicing in the late summer. It is caused by exposure to high heat and humidity, and it can happen to anybody.

What to look for: A person will lose alertness, look pale, and their skin will be cold and clammy.

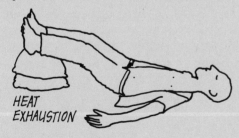

HEAT EXHAUSTION

What to do:
1. The victim should lie down in a shady place.
2. Elevate feet.
3. Loosen clothing.

4. If conscious, have them drink three doses of saltwater. Mix ½ teaspoon of salt to ½ a glass of water.
5. Call a doctor.

To prevent heat exhaustion you should drink plenty of water and eat some salty things. Wear light, loose clothing. Rest when you get hot. Have a shower or bath to cool off.

SUNSTROKE

Sunstroke can happen when a person gets too much sun. Elderly and fat people should be especially careful of sunstroke. Heavy doses of sun on the skull can result in fainting, coma, and even death. Sunstroke is serious!

What to look for: a sunstroke victim will have *hot, dry skin*, dizziness, and a fast, faint heartbeat.

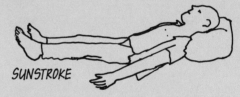

SUNSTROKE

What to do:
1. Move the person to the shade; have them lie down.
2. Elevate the head.
3. Loosen clothing.
4. Sponge victim with cool water.
5. Call a doctor.
6. If conscious, give victim saltwater (check how in Heat Exhaustion section).
7. Fan victim.

To prevent sunstroke stay out of sun and wear a hat.

SCRAPES

Scrapes mean losing the top couple layers of skin and exposing some tiny blood vessels.

What to do:

1. Wash the scrape with soap and water.

2. Get out the ground-in dirt using a clean towel or rag.

3. Some people like to coat a scrape with antiseptic or germ-killing solution. Some people think this is unnecessary.

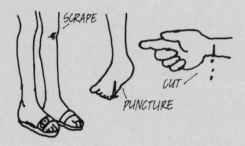

CUTS

Cuts can mean anything from a nick you get from the edge of a piece of paper to something quite serious with loss of much blood.

A little bleeding is a good thing because oozing blood tends to clean a wound and remove dirt and bacteria in the same way a river tends to wash dirt downstream. By the time a scab cap has been formed, the wound has been cleaned.

What to do:

1. A small cut should be given the same treatment as a scrape.

2. A deep cut should be wrapped tightly in cloth until the bleeding stops.

3. If the cut is on an arm or leg, raise that part higher to slow down the bleeding. Once bleeding stops, clean and bandage it.

4. Serious cuts should be checked by a doctor. These are ones with:

— foreign matter (splinters, glass, etc.) too deep to wash out

— a lot of soil contaminated by manure

— hard to stop bleeding

PUNCTURES

Punctures become infected more easily than other types of wounds because it's hard to flush germs and foreign matter out of them.

Tetanus bacteria, especially, spend a lot of time lurking in soil. Once inside a warm, moist place like your body, tetanus bacteria tends to grow. This is a serious problem, so if you get a puncture that is possibly contaminated by dirt, take yourself to a doctor and get ready for a tetanus booster shot.

If you're sure the object that punctured your skin is free of dirt, go ahead and clean the wound yourself. Encourage it to bleed by giving the skin around it a firm pinch and wash and cover it with clean gauze or cloth.

FISH HOOKS

These are made for hooking flesh and not letting go. They are not very discriminating and are equally effective on human flesh as on fish flesh. Once they're in, the tiny barbs make pulling them out a difficult process.

What to do:

1. If the hook is not far in, you can back it out. Then give first aid for a puncture wound.

2. If the hook is in deep enough to be past the barbs, do not try to pull it out. The barbs will tear the flesh and leave a horrible hole. Have a doctor remove it.

3. If there is no doctor to remove it, cut off both ends of the hook and *gently* push the rest of the hook through. Then give first aid for a puncture wound.

BROKEN BONES

If you or a friend should ever bite the dust hard enough to really hurt yourself, or you're not sure, do not try to wiggle the injured part to test whether it's broken or not.

What to do:

First check the injury for these symptoms:

1. The injured part is bent out of shape.
2. There is swelling.
3. It is painful to move.
4. The flesh is broken and bone is poking through.

If you have symptom 4 the arm may be broken in what's called a compound fracture. *Do not* try to push the bones back through the skin. First try to control the bleeding with a sterile cloth or gauze. Call a doctor right away, then treat the victim for shock (see the part about shock — what to do).

BREAKS, STRAINS, AND SPRAINS

If the first three symptoms are happening, the area might be injured in one of these ways:

1. Broken (fractured) or
2. Strained or sprained (this means that the soft tissue which joins the bones together is torn or injured). The first aid treatment is the same for either injury.

What to do:

1. Keep the injured area quiet in a natural position; you may need to prop it up with pillows to support it.
2. Apply an ice pack to the area to slow the swelling.
3. Call a doctor.
4. Treat the patient for shock.

SHOCK

Shock is a body's automatic response to being injured. When it happens, the body's basic functions slow down. Here's what you will notice about a body in shock:

1. The skin gets cold, white, and clammy.
2. Breathing becomes irregular or shallow.
3. The pulse becomes faint and quick.

What to do:

Keep the victim lying down and covered up to protect the body from heat loss.

FOOD POISONING

Sometimes picnic food can make you sick. This can happen when the potato salad or deviled eggs sit around for several hours in a warm place. This tends to happen in summer when food goes outside.

Staphylococci or staph bacteria are carried around by people in the mucous of the nose and throat and on the skin. These bacteria are quick to move into nice *warm* food when it's prepared. If you keep these foods hot or cold — these microcreatures have no chance to grow. Because your warm picnic food is a perfect bacteria incubator, within three to five hours your potato salad is a bowl full of toxin (a toxin is a poison). This can happen to other foods such as: meat, fish, eggs, milk, and milk products (like cream-filled pies).

What to look for:
Three to five hours after eating toxic food, the victim will feel nausea, vomit, have diarrhea and abdominal pain which can last for 24 hours.

What to do:
1. Lie down.
2. Don't eat or drink until the vomiting stops, then have only liquids for a day.
3. Next time make sure cold foods are kept cold and hot foods are kept hot.

POISON OAK, IVY, AND SUMAC

Irritating plants are a real hazard in the summer. It's the time when you're likely to be out clomping around the woods in your shorts. It's a real good idea to know what poison plants look like so you can avoid them. It's not fun spending a couple of hot, itchy weeks trying not to scratch while your friends are out swimming. That's right — those awful, itchy rashes need to be kept high and dry until they heal.

Oh, so you're immune to poison ivy, oak, and sumac? Well the past is no guarantee. Many people start life immune and much to their surprise and dismay find themselves with arms and legs full of itchy bumps after a walk in the woods. Some experts think that you get sensitive to it only after a first-time exposure.

It is possible not to know you're exposed to it. Human skin reacts to the oil produced by these plants. Your dog or cat can pick it up on its fur and then rub up against you. Your mom can pick it up from washing your clothes. The oil is sticky stuff and remains potent. The best protection is to avoid these plants. Learn to recognize them. Here's a lesson in survival botany:

Poison Ivy

Grows everywhere in the USA except California. Looks like a shrub or a vine or a small plant. Has dark green leaves in summer which turn red in fall.

Poison Oak

Grows in California and parts of other western states. Looks like a bush or a vine or a small plant. Like poison ivy, it has green leaves in clusters of three which turn red in the fall.

Poison Sumac

Grows in swampy places mostly in Eastern USA. A woody shrub or small tree 5 to 25 feet tall. Dark green leaves, turning orangey in the fall.

If you plan to hike in places inhabited by these plants, wear long pants and long sleeves. Try not to hug your dog after it returns from a plunge into the underbrush. This is for your protection; poison plants won't bother the dog.

Never burn these plants; the oils can be transmitted in the smoke and contaminate your eyes and lungs.

If you do come in contact with these plants, wash yourself well with soap and water as soon as possible. Then apply rubbing alcohol to the parts of your body which were exposed. Clothing which made contact with the plants should be dry-cleaned. Don't forget to warn the cleaners.

What to look for:

1. Burning, itching — about 24 hours after making contact, sometimes quicker or slower.

2. The area will look red and swollen; then blisters appear.

What to do:

1. Don't scratch. This could break the blisters and spread the rash more.

2. Keep the rash dry.

3. Apply a skin lotion like calamine.

4. Try to keep cool. Working up a sweat makes it itchy and seems to spread it.

5. If you have a severe rash around the eyes, see a doctor.

SNAKEBITES

The vast majority of people bitten by deadly snakes live to tell about it. When you think about it, very few people get bitten. Florida is a state with a large snake population. Each year they average about three bites per 100,000 persons. In America it turns out that chances of surviving a poisonous bite are better than 4000 to 1. Not to say you shouldn't be careful. Your best protection is knowing something about them.

What to look for:

If you have been bitten by a poisonous snake, there will be swelling in the bite area spreading to the rest of the body. You may feel nausea, weakness, numbness, and shock. Full effects come one to two hours after the bite.

What to do:

1. Try to identify the kind of snake.

2. Do everything you can to slow the circulation and prevent the spread of the poison. Lie down with the bite lower than the heart. If you have to walk to help, *move slowly*. Be calm.

3. Put a constricting band a few inches above the bite if it is on an arm or leg. A rolled up handkerchief is fine. It should be snug but *not too tight*. A tight band will cut off circulation, doing more harm than good.

4. Wrap the bite with a damp, cool cloth.

5. Transport the victim to medical help. (If possible have someone go ahead so antivenin will be ready when you arrive.

6. If you're spending time in snake areas, carry a snakebite kit. Know how to use it.

SNAKE HABITS

Three of the four poisonous snakes in our part of North America belong to the same family, called pit vipers. These are the rattlesnake, copperhead, and cottonmouth. They all have a depression or pit under either eye which acts as a heat sensor. This piece of equipment is a handy item for the creatures who make a living hunting warm-blooded creatures. (If you have ever plopped down on a seat recently occupied by a dog, cat, or person, you know how much heat we mammals give off.) All these vipers are thus equipped to find their meals in the dark. They tend to hunt at night, so be careful after twilight. They can sense you, even if you can't see them.

Like all reptiles, snakes have no internal heaters. Snakes tend to be the same temperature as their surroundings. A snake's body needs to be warm to operate well — so a cold snake is a slow snake. And an overheated snake is a dead snake. You are not likely to run into a reptile on a rock top at high noon in the desert. You will find them under things protected from the broiling sun. However they are likely to bask on these warm places to soak up heat after the sun goes down. That's why they are often seen on paved roads late in the day.

Many snakes have adopted a habit of hibernating during the cold, winter months when the drop in temperature makes their lives difficult. They reappear in the spring, hungry after their winter's nap. Their poison glands have had time to recharge, so they are especially dangerous at this time.

THE DEADLY FOUR

You should be able to recognize these so that you can avoid them. If you are bitten, you *need* to know what kind of bite to be treated for. The first-aid book recommends killing the snake so you can bring it along to the doctor. On the next page, they say to stop all muscular activity. It is difficult to kill a snake without moving. My advice is to get a good look at what bit you before one of you retreats.

Rattlesnake — 26 Species, three to eight feet

Most widespread, found in almost all parts of the USA; feeds mostly on mice, rats, and rabbits. It is the most dangerous to man. Because of its large size and accompanying dose of venom, it is described as the boldest and most aggressive of the four. It generally gives a warning signal with its tail before striking humans. When it hunts, it will strike its prey without warning. So it seems the snake, too, senses a dangerous situation and is more than willing to back down. Depending on size and age, this rattle can sound a variety of ways.

Copperhead — three feet long

This is the next most common poisonous snake. It eats mice, large insects, and other snakes. It is found in rocky, hilly, territory and in lower places along walls, hedges, haystacks, and barns. Its camouflage color blends it into the ground and leaves. You're likely to encounter this one stepping over logs.

Cottonmouth or Water Moccasin — three to four feet long with a thick body

This snake lives in watery, swampy places. It feeds on fish, frogs, snakes, lizards, alligators, and birds. The inside of its mouth is a white color and it gives an open mouth warning.

Coral snake — about three feet long at the most

This one has a colorful red on yellow on white pattern with a black swatch. It is a small, thin snake — a cousin to the cobra. It feeds on lizards and other snakes. It is a secretive, burrowing snake.

STINGING NETTLE

The first time you brush up against nettles, you will be surprised with a number of stinging sensations. After the nettles have gotten your attention, you might carefully lift a leaf. The underside is covered with sharp bristles. These are attached to sacs of formic acid — the same nasty stuff you get from an ant sting. It is interesting to note that both the plant and animal kingdom have developed weapons using the same kind of chemical warfare.

What to do:
Nettle stings are not serious. The pain should go away in a short time. Meanwhile dab the area with rubbing alcohol. A bruised dock leaf is supposed to be very soothing. And there are some people who recommend nettle juice itself. This seems like a case of the cure being worse than the disease.

TICKS

These are bugs which make their living by sucking mammal blood. They have mouth parts for puncturing skin and taking sips of your body's own liquid protein. While a little loss of blood isn't a serious matter — you're hardly in danger of being sucked dry by a tick — contamination from their tiny bites can be serious. Ticks can carry spotted fever. Mosquitos are famous for spreading malaria, yellow fever, etc. The best protection is to make yourself as unattractive to these pests as possible. When you're exposed outdoors, use a good insect repellent.

What to do:

If you should pick up a tick, remove it as soon as possible:

1. You can coat it with a heavy oil — salad, mineral, or machine oil — to block its breathing pores. It may come off at once. If not, leave the oil on for 30 minutes then pull the tick off with tweezers. Use a steady pull. Take your time and get all the parts.

2. Wash the area well with soap and water. Dab on some antiseptic.

3. Wash your hands after the operation.

P. S. You can also use this method on your dog.

BITES AND STINGS

Spiders don't sneak around waiting to bite innocent children. Bees don't go out of their way looking for nice plump arms to sink their stingers in. None of these creatures benefit in the least by waging an attack on a hulking human. Indeed, bees die soon after losing their stingers — and spiders are likely to get the worst of any battle with a human.

Most creatures have to feel that their nests, babies, or lives are in great danger before they turn their weapons on you. So if you are careful where you put your feet and hands and treat other creatures with care and respect, keeping a healthy distance from them, you should never have to use the following first aid.

HOW TO RESPECT A SPIDER

There are about 2,500 kinds of spiders in the North American continent — not counting Mexico. Only two kinds are harmful to humans.

Without spiders, life on earth would be overrun with insects. However, when some people meet up with a spider, they only seem to remember the troublesome two. It is estimated that each year the world's spiders eat enough insects to outweigh the earth's entire human population. If you think about how many mosquitos it would take to equal your own weight, perhaps you would be a little friendlier to spiders.

SPIDER BITES

All spiders produce a little venom. Only the black widow and the brown recluse spider produce poison capable of making humans sick. Ordinary spider bites are not too serious. They may cause a swelling and burning at the bite site, plus some sweating, nausea, and cramps. They are painful but seldom fatal.

What to do:

1. Tie a constricting band above bites on legs and arms for five to ten minutes.

2. Keep this area lower than the heart.

3. Apply ice to the area.

4. Call a doctor.

SPIDERS TO AVOID

Black Widow

Found all over the United States and Southern Canada. The female is large enough to bite. She has a red, hourglass-shaped mark on her belly. They're found in dark corners, under logs, etc. Florida's widow is brown with a red hourglass.

Brown Recluse

Found in southern and central U. S. A. This spider has a violin-shaped mark on its head along its six eyes. It is shy, living under rock and the bark of trees.

Tarantula

This is a large, hairy-looking spider that roams on the ground. The bite of this ferocious looking spider is not poisonous. The pain comes from the wound made by their powerful jaws, though most people suffer symptoms no more

serious than an ordinary bee sting. These spiders, too, are shy creatures and like nothing better than to be left alone.

INSECT STINGS

For most people, insect stings are painful summer hazards, but nothing very serious. This section is for them.

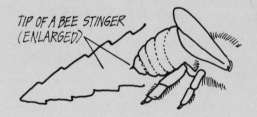

TIP OF A BEE STINGER (ENLARGED)

There are other people for whom bees and wasps present a deadly problem. Their bodies are supersensitive to the poison in their stings. In fact, bee stings kill more people than snakebites — and it can happen more quickly. A person who is sensitive should warn their outdoor companions about their problem and introduce them to their insect allergy kit.

Now for the rest of you.

What to do:

The first problem is to remove the stinger. Scrape it away. Don't try to pick it out because you might squeeze the sac, pumping more poison into your skin.

1. Use ice on the area.

2. Sometimes a paste of baking soda is soothing.

3. Some people like to plaster mud on the area.

HUMAN BITES

Don't laugh. Any break in your skin is a break in your body's defenses. Human mouths have more kinds of bacteria living in them than dog mouths. So if your little brother bites you, don't forget to treat it.

ANIMAL BITES

You should always take care when handling wild animals. Even though there are no poisonous mammals, their bites can carry diseases like rabies and tetanus.

Stay clear of any wild animal that acts really friendly. Friendly behavior isn't normal for wild animals. There's a chance that the animal has rabies, a disease which affects the brain in its later stages. If you are bitten by such an animal, don't take chances. *See a doctor.*

What to do:

1. Wash the wound well with soap and water.

2. Flush it with lots of water.

3. Cover it with a sterile pad

DOG BITES

If you are bitten by a dog, you will need to find the dog's owner. The animal will have to be kept for observation to see if it has rabies. Wash the wound and talk to your doctor.

SEND AWAY:

FIRST-AID GUIDE

Johnson and Johnson, the people who make Band-Aids, produce a little book called, "First Aid Guide." It tells what to do in emergencies, how to bandage and move the injured, and it contains a fold-out wall chart. Hang it over your bed to study before you go to sleep at night, or post it near the medicine chest.

Johnson and Johnson
501 George Street
New Brunswick, New Jersey
08903

P. S. A younger brother or sister might be interested in a guide called "First Aid for Little People," for kids in the first to third grades. Also available from Johnson and Johnson.

10
CRAFTS

SOAP CARVING

Maybe you would like to try whittling, but you are not sure you want to invest your savings in a pocketknife. Here is a way to get the feel of carving without having to spend more than the price of a bar of soap.

Get a bar of white hand soap; use a sharp paring knife from the kitchen. Don't use a serrated blade. It won't leave a smooth slice. A nail file might also be helpful.

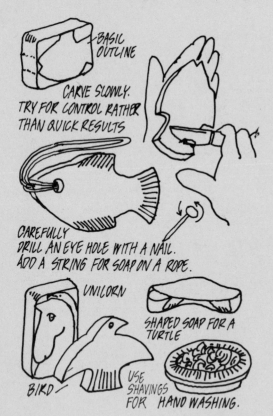

BASIC OUTLINE

CARVE SLOWLY.
TRY FOR CONTROL RATHER THAN QUICK RESULTS

CAREFULLY DRILL AN EYE HOLE WITH A NAIL. ADD A STRING FOR SOAP ON A ROPE.

UNICORN

SHAPED SOAP FOR A TURTLE

BIRD

USE SHAVINGS FOR HAND WASHING.

1. Work on a sheet of newspaper so that you don't make a mess.

2. Draw the basic shape onto the bar of soap.

3. Cut away the big sections you don't need.

4. Refine the shape by cutting away with little strokes. Finish shaping with a file.

5. Use the knife point for details and lines.

6. Paint your carving with watercolors if you like.

When you finish you might want to try your hand at whittling with wood. Soft woods like pine, fir, or redwood are easiest to whittle. Read the next section to see how to get your knife in shape.

POCKETKNIFE

Back in the days when your gramp was a lad, a pocketknife was a prized possession. Evry kid knew how to play mumblety peg, make whistles, and whittle. These days a lot of the art of the pocketknife is lost. Coming up is an introduction to one of the handiest, pocket-sized friends a kid ever had.

THERE ARE ALL KINDS OF KNIVES

Pen knife. Lightweight blade, originally got it's name as a tool for cutting points on quill pens.

Souvenir knife. Keep it with your keepsakes. It won't cut.

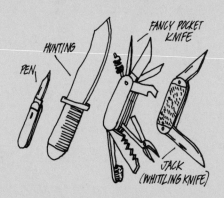

Hunting knife. Good for camping, cleaning fish, fixing meals. Your all-purpose, heavy-duty knife.

Pocketknife that sings and dances. You've seen these kind with a saw, can opener, bottle uncorker, leather punch, scissors, and the kitchen sink. Great for people in the Swiss army or great for getting stranded on a desert island.

Jackknife. Just the tool for whittling. One big blade and a smaller one for finer details.

You can spend anywhere from $2 to $20 for a whittling knife. What do you get for all that extra money? More expensive knives have better qualities.

What to look for; don't buy one with stainless steel blades. Once they get dull, you can't sharpen them. Carbon steel is what you want.

Hold the knife up. Cheaper ones sometimes show the light of day behind them.

A good knife shouldn't have any wiggle. The blade should feel good and solid.

A better knife will hold a sharpened edge longer, because it is a harder metal. A cheap knife will wear out more quickly due to extra sharpening.

CARE AND FEEDING OF A KNIFE

To get the best results, your knife needs to be in tiptop shape. Every so often give it a dab of oil at the joints, so it doesn't get arthritic.

To sharpen it you will need a whet or sharpening stone. A small one is fine for a jackknife. You can buy one at a hardware store. Each stone is a little different. Some need to be used with a little water or a piddle of oil for best results. Read the instructions that come with the stone. Generally this is what you do.

1. Rub the cutting edge against the stone. The knife should be held at an angle.

2. Use a back and forth motion or a circular motion, whichever gets you the best results.

3. Turn the blade over and sharpen the other side.

4. Wipe the blade clean. Polish it off on your shoe bottom.

It should take about a minute of work to keep a knife in condition, if you do it often enough. Once you let it get dull, count on about twenty minutes of grinding time. A sharp knife should cut through a pencil-sized twig in one stroke.

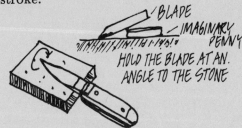

BLADE
IMAGINARY PENNY
HOLD THE BLADE AT AN ANGLE TO THE STONE

KNIFE KNOW-HOW

Keep it sharp. A dull knife needs lots of pressure to make it cut. A sharp knife bites right into the wood.

A dull knife tends to slip off the wood, and slips with a knife are dangerous.

Never cut toward yourself.

Fold up the blade when it is not in use.

Don't throw it. This is bad for the knife.

Use common sense, it's sharp.

EASY PROJECTS WITH YOUR POCKETKNIFE

Itching to put your knife to the test? Here are a couple more simple projects you can make to have fun with.

LEAPERS

This is a simple toy that even the newest whittler can make. You need a Y-shaped twig and a rubber band.

1. Trim a branch to a Y shape with your knife.

2. Cut a straight piece of stick a couple of inches long.

3. Put your leaper together like the picture. Twist up the rubber band so that it is really tight.

4. Put your wound-up leaper on the ground gently. Stand clear and watch it leap. You might have to give it a gentle nudge with another stick. You can have faster, higher, farther contests with other leapers in your neighborhood.

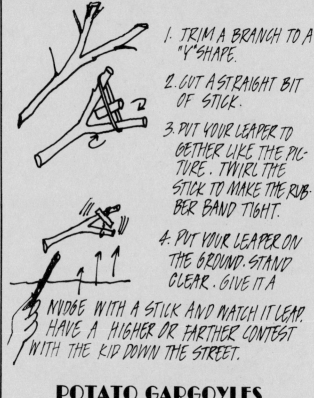

1. TRIM A BRANCH TO A "Y" SHAPE.

2. CUT A STRAIGHT BIT OF STICK.

3. PUT YOUR LEAPER TOGETHER LIKE THE PICTURE. TWIRL THE STICK TO MAKE THE RUBBER BAND TIGHT.

4. PUT YOUR LEAPER ON THE GROUND. STAND CLEAR. GIVE IT A NUDGE WITH A STICK AND WATCH IT LEAP. HAVE A HIGHER OR FARTHER CONTEST WITH THE KID DOWN THE STREET.

POTATO GARGOYLES

A gargoyle is not something you do for a sore throat. A gargoyle is a stone demon that was attached to cathedrals to frighten away evil. You can carve your own gargoyle out of a potato that will shrivel and dry to look like it was made out of stone. Use it to frighten away anything you like.

CARVE AWAY A FACE:

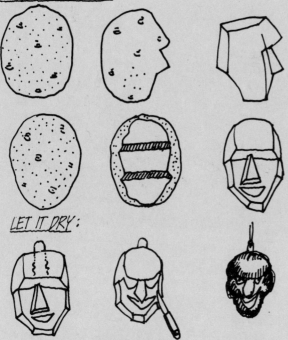

LET IT DRY:

1. Start with a big potato.
2. Cut away chunks to form a nose, mouth, and forehead. Carve some eyes. Add some ears.
3. Remove any pieces of peel left on your gargoyle.
4. Stick a wire through the carving. Hang it in a warm place to dry.
5. As it dries, it will shrivel up. You can still mold it with your fingers and carve away bits as it dries.

POUCH

Here is a neat little pouch you can weave to wear around your neck. It will hold all sorts of important things like gum money, marbles, or tree frogs. It is fast to weave and fun to make.

You will need:
8 yards of T-shirt yarn
a 4x5-inch piece of stiff cardboard
about 5 yards of heavy cotton string or
rug yarn
a bit of plastic from a bottle

Before you start weaving you need to make a needle. Cut it from a plastic bottle. Punch a hole in one end so you can thread the T-shirt yarn through it.

Now to start weaving:

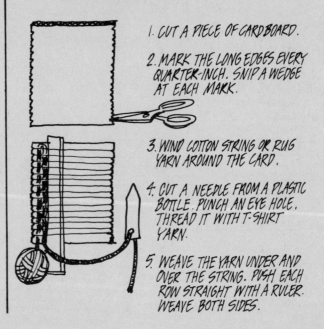

1. CUT A PIECE OF CARDBOARD.

2. MARK THE LONG EDGES EVERY QUARTER-INCH. SNIP A WEDGE AT EACH MARK.

3. WIND COTTON STRING OR RUG YARN AROUND THE CARD.

4. CUT A NEEDLE FROM A PLASTIC BOTTLE. PUNCH AN EYE HOLE. THREAD IT WITH T-SHIRT YARN.

5. WEAVE THE YARN UNDER AND OVER THE STRING. PUSH EACH ROW STRAIGHT WITH A RULER. WEAVE BOTH SIDES.

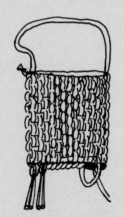

6. SLIDE THE WEAVING OFF THE CARD. SEW UP THE BOTTOM WITH LEFTOVER YARN END.

7. LOOP THE OTHER LEFTOVER END AROUND FOR A HANDLE.

8. ADD FRINGE TO THE BOTTOM IF YOU LIKE.

READ "WILD COLOR" TO FIND OUT HOW TO MAKE T-SHIRT YARN. YOU WILL NEED ABOUT 7 YARDS.

WILD COLOR

Before you weave you might want to try your hand at dyeing your string or T-shirt yarn with some wild dyes. No doubt there are some things in your kitchen or yard that you could squeeze some color out of:

WALNUT HULLS	RICH BROWN
SPINACH	YELLOW GREEN
TEA	GOLDEN TAN
COFFEE	BROWN
ONION SKINS	YELLOW:GOLD/RED:RED
BERRIES	VARIOUS PINKS, REDS
MARIGOLDS	BROWN GREEN

The brightest natural colors are gotten on wool yarn, though cotton works too. First soak the yarn in water so it is wet all through. Then simmer it in the dyebath until you get a deep color. Remove the yarn and hang it up to dry.

Read on to find out how to make the dyebath.

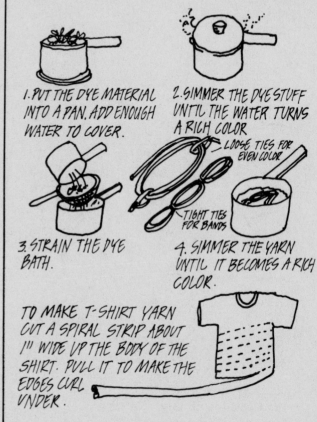

1. PUT THE DYE MATERIAL INTO A PAN. ADD ENOUGH WATER TO COVER.

2. SIMMER THE DYE STUFF UNTIL THE WATER TURNS A RICH COLOR

3. STRAIN THE DYE BATH.

4. SIMMER THE YARN UNTIL IT BECOMES A RICH COLOR.

LOOSE TIES FOR EVEN COLOR

TIGHT TIES FOR BANDS

TO MAKE T-SHIRT YARN CUT A SPIRAL STRIP ABOUT 1" WIDE UP THE BODY OF THE SHIRT. PULL IT TO MAKE THE EDGES CURL UNDER.

SALT CLAY

Salt clay is a lot like sand clay. The cornstarch binds the small particles into a mass you can mold and dry. It is a bit easier to mold than sand clay and will dry white.

You will need:
1 cup table salt
¾ cup cold water
½ cup cornstarch
double boiler
wooden spoon
wax paper

To make it:

1. Combine the cornstarch and salt in the top of the double boiler.

2. Pour in the water. Put on the heat, stirring constantly.

3. After several minutes this liquid hardens to dough. This happens really fast.

4. When it reaches dough state slap it on some wax paper.

5. As soon as it's cool enough to handle, knead it for about 2 minutes to get the lumps out. Here's how:

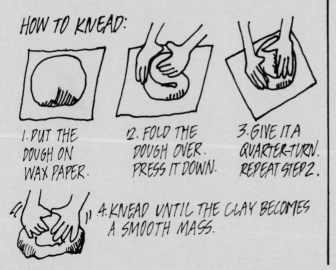

HOW TO KNEAD:

1. PUT THE DOUGH ON WAX PAPER.

2. FOLD THE DOUGH OVER. PRESS IT DOWN.

3. GIVE IT A QUARTER-TURN. REPEAT STEP 2.

4. KNEAD UNTIL THE CLAY BECOMES A SMOOTH MASS.

To mold it:

6. Mold it to animals, beads, pinch pots. Try not to make anything fat that will have a hard time drying.

7. It will dry hard. You can paint it or draw on it with a felt marker.

8. Extra clay can be stored in an airtight coffee can with a lid or a double plastic bag. Throw in a damp sponge to keep it moist.

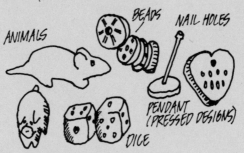

WORK QUICKLY! CLAY DRIES FAST.

ANIMALS

BEADS

NAIL HOLES

PENDANT (PRESSED DESIGNS)

DICE

SEARCH FOR SALT

Salt, to most people in our part of the world, is something to sprinkle on popcorn. We don't give salt a thought. Why, next to dirt, it's about the cheapest thing you can buy. But getting enough salt in some parts of the world can be a real problem.

The early settlers in America found salt scarce and expensive. It might cost as much as $10.00 a barrel. In those days $10.00 could equal a month's wages. At this price, many families would make do with about a pound a year. (It was certainly too precious to squander fooling around making salt clay.)

It's no accident that the oldest city in Ohio is built on salt springs. The Europeans found the Indians collecting salt from the springs. They called the spot Shaneetown and went into the salt business themselves. At one time, this place produced 20,000 bushels of salt per year.

In 1965 a writer for National Geographic traveled with a salt caravan through the Sahara. He learned that salt comes from pits outside of a town called Bilma in Niger. It is cast into unwieldy 40 pound molds, then loaded onto camels. Every winter the Tuareg, nomad people of the desert, move these blocks of salt 300 miles across the savage Sahara. Its destination is a town where salt is scarce. Here it sells for 10 times the original price.

Salt is a necessary part of our diet. Lacking salt, the cells in your body don't work. Salt can be a matter of life and death.

SALT TEST

Ever wonder just how salty the ocean is? If you live near the ocean or are visiting, you can find out first hand.

Here's how:

1. Boil 1 cup of sea water until all the water evaporates.

2. What's left? What does it taste like? The ocean has been called a weak solution of just about everything. About 80 percent of the salt left in your pot is sodium chloride — what we call table salt. To a scientist, salt is a dissolved chemical. There in the pot you have some potassium, some magnesium, some iron, some calcium, some copper, some cobalt, some. . .

SEND AWAY:
SALTY TALES

Did you know that all water is a little bit salty?

Some parts of the oceans are saltier than others.

If you could evaporate the earth's oceans, there would be enough salt to spread a 500 foot layer over the land.

You can get all this and more information in a booklet called "Why is the Ocean Salty?" It's free from:

U. S. Department of the Interior
Geological Survey
1200 South Eads Street
Arlington, Virginia
22202

SAND-CASTING

This is a fun project to do at a beach or a lake or anywhere there is a good supply of sand. You can't decide to do sandcasting at the last second because you need some special tools down there at the beach.

You will need:
About 5 pounds of plaster of paris. You can buy this at a hardware store or building supply.
A big tin can for mixing the plaster. A big coffee tin is good.
Stirring stick.
Knives, spoons, and assorted kitchen tools for making the mold.

P. S. You might bring along some extra plaster. When I did this, every kid on the beach wanted to try.

CUTAWAY VIEW   LOOKING DOWN INTO THE MOLD

POUR IN THE PLASTER

DIG IT UP AND CLEAN

Here is what to do:

1. Find a flat sandy spot. The sand should be damp. Check over your shoulder to make sure your spot won't be flooded by the tide in the next 20 minutes.

2. Set to work digging your mold. You will have to form whatever you are making in reverse. So parts that stick out, like a nose, have to be dug *into* the sand.

Use your fingers or tools to press or poke some textures into the sand.

3. Build a ridge of sand around your mold to hold the liquid plaster.

4. Gently pour in the plaster so that it fills your dug-out sculpture. It should cover a bit of the lip.

5. Let it dry. It should harden in about 15 minutes.

6. When it's dry dig it up. Careful! The plaster tends to crack easily at this stage. Brush or wash away the sand. It should be fully dry in about a day.

Use a seashell, some sandpaper, or a knife to carve a more finished shape or to add some details. You can paint your casting and give it a coat of shine with shellac.

HOW TO MIX PLASTER

A large sized coffee can filled about a third full of water should mix enough plaster to fill a sneaker-sized mold. This is a good size for a trial run.

1. Fill the container with the amount of liquid you think it will take to fill your mold.

2. Pour the plaster of paris into the water. You know you have enough when a little mountain forms in the center.

3. Stir slowly with your fingers or a stick.

4. It is ready to pour when it is the thickness of thin gravy. Don't wait around, it dries fast!

Hints:

Saltwater makes it harden faster than fresh. So does stirring it quickly.

A little vinegar slows down the drying process. Never pour plaster down the drains.

You can chip the mixing can clean when the wet plaster dries.

PLASTER OF PARIS

What is this weird stuff that turns from soup to rock?

It is actually a ground up mineral called gypsum. When it is mixed with water into a paste, it dries into a solid mass of interlocking crystals — sort of like when water turns to ice.

Gypsum is a soft, whitish mineral. It is often dissolved in water and it concentrates where water has been, like in the dried remains of lakes, or as stalactites or stalagmites in caves. There are some famous gypsum flowers in Limestone Caves, Kentucky. Gypsum is mined all over the world.

You will be glad to know that gypsum is used by dentists and doctors for making casts and as an ingredient in making paint. Sometimes it even finds its way into candy as a filler.

And why is it called plaster of paris? Because once, centuries ago, a deposit of this material was found outside this city.

PLASTER OF PARIS PRINTS

Buy a small amount of plaster of paris from a hobby store. Collect an old bucket or can, a stirring stick, small boxes or paper cups, and a nail.

For printing you'll need printer's ink or thick tempera paint and paper.

1. Assemble all the equipment and work fast. Put one pint of water in container. Gradually add plaster to water, a big spoonful at a time. Break up the lumps and stir. When the mixture looks thick like whipping cream it's ready to pour.

2. Quickly pour plaster in boxes or cups. In 10 minutes the block will be ready to design with the nail. Press and scratch the design into the block, then leave it to dry for about 3 hours.

PAPER CUPS

SMOOTH THE PLASTER WITH A KNIFE.

CUT AWAY MILK CARTON

FINISHED PRINT

PAINT THE STAMP

CLOTH PAPER

PRINTING

1. Cover the block with paint or ink using a brush.

2. Carefully lay paper flat on top, and without moving, press paper down with a soft cloth.

3. Peel paper away carefully and there is your print.

SAND CLAY

Here is your chance to make mud pies on the stove. Better get permission first. Don't choose the best pots in the house. Sand has a tendency to be rough on stuff, leaving a lot of tiny little scratches.

You will need:
1 cup sand
½ cup cornstarch (from the supermarket)
½ cup boiling water
a double boiler
a wooden spoon
Got everything ready? Then proceed:

1. Mix up the dry sand and cornstarch.
2. Pour in the boiling water.
3. Cook the mess over a double boiler. Stir it constantly until it gets thick. (This won't take long.)
4. Let it cool.

In the wet state it looks like something that your mother would yell at you for bringing into the house. Don't be alarmed. It will look really yucky until it dries. Then it looks the same color as the original sand with a nice hard surface.

5. You can mold your sand clay into beads or animals, whatever takes your fancy.
6. Cook the clay in the oven. 300 degrees is about right. Cook until it's dry.
7. Now is your chance to sweep the kitchen. Sand all over the place has a way of getting under a mother's skin.
8. You might coat the clay with a coat of lacquer to prevent flaking.

Here are some hints for working with sand clay. If the clay isn't sticking together, add more water. You can make a finer clay with finer sand. Sift the sand through several layers of window screen or cheesecloth.

Sand comes in all colors. Start a collection of different colored sands from different places. Make them into earth beads of many colors. String them and wear them.

LOOKING AT SAND

If you have ever looked at sand closely you know it is made up of tiny bits of rock. Also you may have noticed that sand is usually found close to water or where water has been. You may be surprised to know that sand is a lot of rocks worn out by water.

You can buy sand for your sand clay at the garden shop or you can go out and prospect for your own. You will see it at the ocean side and along stream beds or lake shores. You will find sand being made wherever water acts on rocks.

Waves are famous for making sand. The sea acts as a sideways saw, cutting into cliffs. Every so often a cliff face collapses to be chewed into cobbles by the waves. You can hear the grinding at any beach.

Running water acts as a knife, cutting valleys into the land. Banks fall into the water and are ground into pebbles along the bottom. Pebbles are worn into sandy bits which are carried along and dumped in the slower moving, shallow places. You can notice this natural sorting where sands of different sizes appear together in different places along a shore. A bit of observation and some careful thinking can tell you a lot about how they got there.

Sometimes sand is found in places far from any water. These can be old river or lake beds or desert sands. Of course not all deserts are sandy. In fact ¾ of the world's deserts are bare rock and gravel, not a promising site for the making of new sands. It is likely that desert sand was made by the action of ancient seas or the cutting action of wind on sandstone cliffs. Sometimes desert winds will pile sand up into dunes. This sand will become very fine as it gets worn by knocking into other particles.

STONE SCULPTURE

This is a good thing to do when you're near an ocean or lake. Sit yourself down with a good supply of stones. Pick one up and look at it.

Chances are there is a person or animal right there in the rock. Use a pen or brush to complete the sculpture.

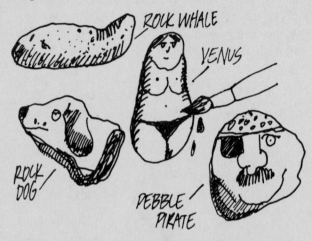

Try another. You will find it is a bit like eating popcorn; once you get started, it is hard to stop. Wolves, seals, seagulls, executives, and trolls will be lurking everywhere.

If you do a piece you want to save, give it a coat of liquid wax.

11
SWIMMING

SWIMMING

For a lot of kids the best part of summer is the time spent at the beach, on a lake, or wading in a stream. Water is especially magic on a hot day. No doubt you will be spending some of your summertime around water. This section is a collection of stuff to do near or in a body of water.

GONE FISHING

You don't need a fancy fishing pole to catch fish. In fact you don't need a fishing pole at all. You can catch fish with a simple handline that you can make yourself. When you finish, you will have a fishing outfit that fits in your pocket and works. All you need to buy are the hooks.

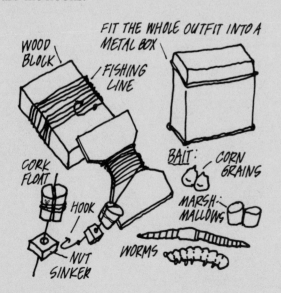

WOOD BLOCK

FIT THE WHOLE OUTFIT INTO A METAL BOX

FISHING LINE

CORK FLOAT

HOOK

NUT SINKER

BAIT: CORN GRAINS

MARSH-MALLOWS

WORMS

SEND AWAY:

POKE POLING

This is the kind of fishing you can do in rocky, intertidal ocean areas. If you live near such a place or if you are planning to visit one this summer, you might want to try it. You can build your own pole from stuff around the house. If it sounds like something you might want to try, write for the sheet called "Poke Pole Fishing." It's from:

Publications
University of California
Division of Agricultural Sciences
1422 South 10th Street
Richmond, California
94804

SEND AWAY:

GYOTAKU, OR ALL THE FISH THAT'S FIT TO PRINT

Caught a whopper? You can make a print of the monster to back up your fish story. Or maybe you caught something a little smaller. Well, you can print the fish and brag about the print. All fish prints are beautiful, even ones made from your recently deceased goldfish at home.

Gyotaku is the art of Japanese fish printing. It also works for rocks and flowers. You can learn how to do it from a leaflet published by the University of California Extension Service. It is free from:

Publications
University of California
Division of Agricultural Sciences
1422 South 10th Street
Richmond, California
94804

Ask for AXT-445-3, "Gyotaku, Japanese Fish Printing."

FLOATING

Drop a piece of bone into water and it sinks. Drop a slice of steak and it sinks. You are muscles and bones. How come you float when you are dropped in the water?

If you think about it carefully, you will remember that all of you doesn't float. When you were on your back, remember how your feet kept sinking? The part of you that sits right up out of the water is your chest. Inside your chest are your lungs. These air-filled bags act like a couple of inside life preservers, keeping your body afloat.

You can feel the change in your floatability every time you breathe. Next time you are in some water, take a deep breath. Feel yourself rise in the water? Now, breathe out, feel yourself sink? Lucky for you there is no way to empty your lungs of all their air. You are unsinkable.

FLOATERS

Here are a couple of ideas for things you can make to float around with. Maybe you can think of some more ideas. Look around your house for things that hold air.

OLD AIR MATTRESS

HOLD WAIST END SHUT.

HEAVY-DUTY-PLASTIC-BAG TRAPPED AIR

EMERGENCY FLOATERS—A PAIR OF PANTS WITH KNOTTED LEGS

MAKE A SIT DOWN FLOAT WITH TWO INNER TUBES.

1. CUT ONE FOR THE SEAT. PUNCH HOLES. ATTACH CORDS.

2. TIE THE SEAT ONTO AN INFLATED TUBE.

HOLEY THINGS

Every once in a while you come across an object with a hole in it. Not often, but sometimes a holey rock or shell or bone turns up. Beaches are especially good places to find holey things. If you find one, save it. You can string it and wear it on a leather thong or on a piece of cord. With a little patience you might find enough pieces for a whole bracelet or necklace full of weird objects. There is no hurry. Looking is half the fun.

ROCK SKIPPING

You can't do it just any place, you need a body of calm water with a nearby supply of flat stones. Maybe you know of a place like that. Or maybe you'll just find yourself at such a spot sometime. Finding such a place is a little like finding a present, because skipping stones is a good time.

Here's a lesson in throwing stones:

The perfect skipping stone is flat on both sides and it has rounded edges.

It's not too heavy and not too light. You should be able to give it a good snap when you throw it.

THE PERFECT STONE:

THE GRIP:

THE IDEAL THROW:

The grip:

1. Steady it with your thumb and forefinger.

2. Hold it so you can give it some high speed and lots of spin.

The ideal throw:

1. It should fly low over the water, with the flat side of the stone next to the water's surface.

2. It should have lots of snap so the stone has speed and spin.

STONED PHYSICS

So how come sometimes a rock will skip along the water and other times it goes plop?

Anybody who has ever done a belly flop has some clues to answering this question. You know that when you hit the water flat out, it hurts. The water hits you with a lot of resistance.

When you dive into the water, your body cuts into the surface, and the water slips right around your long, thin shape.

When you throw a flat rock along the water, the flat surface slaps the water rather than digs in. If you throw it hard enough it will slap the surface and glance off. The water doesn't have time to give way and swallow up the skipping stone. The stone will gradually slow down. It will sink when it touches the surface long enough for the water to be pushed aside.

Time for another try.

STONE STORIES

It's no accident that nature often places a good supply of skipping stones next to a body of water.

Skipping stones and pebbles are chunks of rock that have broken away from a larger piece. Pebbles are rocks with all their edges knocked off by wind or more often by water. You can see pebbles being made along beaches, where waves wash a chunk of rock in the sand, grinding it down until it is nothing but sand itself. Rivers, especially the fast moving kind, are good at making pebbles.

EVEN GRAINED

LAYERED

CYLINDERS ARE MADE FROM ROCKS THAT BREAK INTO LONG NARROW PIECES.

If you start looking at pebbles seriously, you will notice that they are hard little lumps. That's because the softies don't last long. Pebbles can be made out of any kind of rock or mineral. Even diamonds and rubies have been found in pebble form. Some pebbles are round all over. Some are flat with rounded edges. Round pebbles are made from stones with an even grain. They wear down equally all around.

Flat pebbles are made of rock with an uneven grain. Rocks that were made by the pressure of layer upon layer of material are denser in one direction and will wear into flat rocks — the good kind for skipping.

LIKE A ROLLING STONE

While you were picking up stones for skipping, did you notice anything about their whereabouts? If you've never thought about a shore, you might think it would be a topsy-turvy place with all that crashing and bashing water. The opposite is true. A beach is a very orderly place because of the action of water.

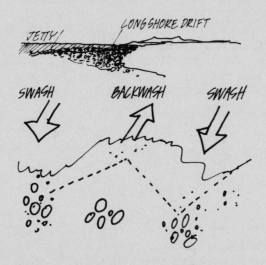

Any stone skipper who pays attention knows that beach rocks are sorted according to size. The heaviest are at the top.

Wait a minute, the top? You would think the heaviest and hardest-to-move rocks would get stuck at the bottom. Right?

Wrong. Wave action hits the beach with a lot of force. This is called swash. The backwash is much weaker. The result is that the big heavy rocks are lifted to the top. The backwash isn't strong enough to carry them back. They sit stranded at the top of the beach. This is how beaches sort themselves out.

Meanwhile the tinies roll back down. Usually waves don't hit a shore straight on. So the rocks move up along the beach at an angle and roll back down. The constant swash and backwash really move the smaller rocks along. You can see them pile up alongside of jettys. Sometimes whole beaches get up and gradually drift away.

SETTING STONES

While you are out picking up stones for skipping, keep your eyes peeled for pretty pebbles that you might want to wear. Here is a simple way to make a bracelet out of your pebbles when you get home. All you need is some metal sheeting, like copper, that you can cut with heavy scissors or tin snips. You can get it at a hardware or hobby store.

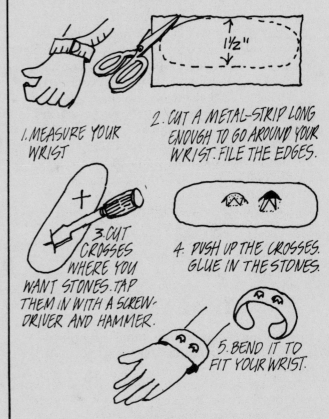

GAMES ON THE FLAT

The games coming up are board games, but you don't need a board to play them. Play anywhere there is a flat spot where you can scratch a playing space into the earth or draw one on a piece of cardboard. The world is full of things that can be markers. Look for things like shells, pebbles, nuts, sticks, bottle caps.

You can pick up and play anywhere, but beaches are especially good places.

YOTÉ

This is a West African game that is sometimes played for stakes. A board is usually scooped out in the earth. Sticks and stones are the playing pieces. You can make an indoor version with a couple of egg cartons.

Get ready:

Scoop out a board like the picture. The two players get twelve pieces each, sticks vs. stones.

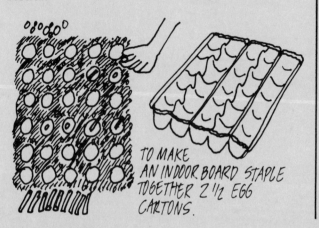

TO MAKE AN INDOOR BOARD STAPLE TOGETHER 2 1/2 EGG CARTONS.

To play:

1. Pebbles starts by putting his piece in any hole.

2. Sticks does the same. Only one piece may be played each turn. Only one marker is allowed in a space at a time. All the sticks and stones do not have to be played before the pieces on the board can be moved.

3. Pieces on the board can be moved one space in a straight line. (Diagonal moves are cheating).

4. Pieces are captured by jumping them and removing them from the board. (The same as in checkers). The jumper is then allowed a bonus capture of the other player's piece from anywhere on the board.

PUZZLE

Make a standing up cross with six markers like the diagram. Make it into a lying down cross by moving just one marker. Can't be done? Oh yes it can. If you don't believe it turn the page for the solution.

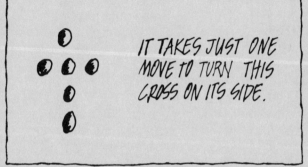

IT TAKES JUST ONE MOVE TO TURN THIS CROSS ON ITS SIDE.

PUZZLE ANSWER: MOVE THE BOTTOM MARKER AROUND TO BECOME THE BASE OF THE LYING DOWN CROSS.

MEMORY

Get ready:
Each player draws a board and gathers a set of ten markers such as stones or twigs.

How to play:

1. One player arranges his markers in a mixed up way over his board.

2. When all the markers are in position the board is unveiled to the other players. They have seven seconds to memorize the way the board looks.

3. Then they rush to their boards and try to duplicate the original with their own equipment.

You can score the game all or nothing. Another way is to chalk up points: one point for each position right, minus one for each position wrong.

THREE-IN-A-ROW

Get ready:
First draw a Three-in-a-Row board. Each player will need three markers. Position them as shown in the picture.

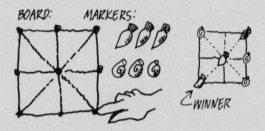

How to play:
This game is something like Tic-Tac-Toe. The object is to move your markers to form a line of three.

1. Toss to see who moves first.

2. Markers can only be moved one jump at a time to a neighboring crossroads. Jumping over markers is not allowed.

NINES

Here is a game you can play alone.
Get ready:
Draw a square board. Divide it into 25 spaces like the picture. Place nine markers on the inside squares.

How to play:
The object is to remove all but a marker left in the middle square. You can remove a marker by jumping it like in checkers. Multiple jumps are fair.

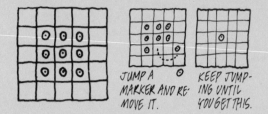

JUMP A MARKER AND RE-MOVE IT.

KEEP JUMP-ING UNTIL YOU GET THIS.

You can play against yourself by trying to make fewer moves. It is rumored that a four move game is possible. What do you think?

KNUCKLE BONES

In ancient Greece, Knuckle Bones was play-ed to foretell the future. You might have run into this game right on the playground. These days it goes by the name of Jacks.

Here is how to play the old way. Find five stones or bones. Do the following to see who plays first.

1. Hold the bones in your palm.

2. Toss them up and catch as many as you can on the back of your hand. Count them.

3. Toss them up from the back of your hand, catching them in your palm. Add the sur-vivors to your first count. Whoever scores the most goes first.

Knuckle Bones is a series of games. You play until you miss. Then your opponent takes over and trys to outplay you.

To play Pickups:

1. Toss out four of the bones. The one you save is called the jack.

2. Toss up the jack. While it is in flight pick up a bone and catch it on the way down. Move it over to your free hand.

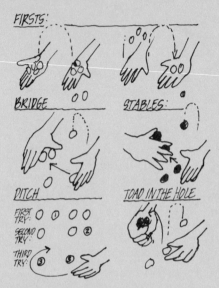

FIRSTS:

BRIDGE

STABLES:

DITCH

FIRST TRY:
SECOND TRY:
THIRD TRY:

TOAD IN THE HOLE

3. Pick up all the bones one by one. Then two by two. Then three plus one. Then four at once.

To play Under-the-Bridge:

1. Form an archway with your hand. Flick in the pieces one at a time while the jack is in the air. Move on to twos, threes, and fours.

To play Stables:

1. With your palm down flat spread your fingers to make stables. Push the bones in the spaces between your fingers.

2. Now remove them.

To play The Ditch:

1. Line up the bones a couple inches apart.

2. Pick up the first.

3. Pick up the third.

4. Pick up the last two.

To play Toad-in-the-Hole.

1. Make your hand into a tunnel. Toss your bones into the hole.

12
THE
CONSERVATION KID

THE CONSERVATION KID

The environment is a little like the weather. Everybody complains about it, but hardly anyone does anything to make it any better. Because you're a kid is no reason to think that you can't do anything to help. Kids can be very powerful people. This section has some things any kid can do.

SOME FACTS

Yeh, so big deal, what can one person do? How can what I do possibly make any difference? Here are some facts:

A small water leak which fills a coffee cup in ten minutes wastes 3,280 gallons of water in a year.

If everybody in America washed clothes in warm or cold water instead of hot, 100,000 barrels of oil could be saved daily. (A barrel of oil equals one man at hard labor for two years.)

A 60-watt bulb burning for one year costs the earth 600 pounds of coal.

118 pounds of newspaper equals one tree. (There are 17 trees to a ton.) Weigh a week's worth of newspapers to get an idea of how many trees your family uses per month.

An aluminum can more than half full of gasoline equals the energy it takes to make that can. That's a lot of fuel to sit around unrecycled.

America's air conditioners use more electricity in a year than all the people in China do.

STUFF YOU CAN DO RIGHT NOW

Put a jug of water in the fridge, so you'll always have an instant supply of cold water without having to run the faucet.

Fill up two quart-sized plastic bottles with water. Set them in the tank above the toilet. Every time you flush, they will save the amount of water in the bottles.

Turn off some of the juice: any lights, radios, televisions on that aren't being used.

Have a shower instead of a bath. Showers take less water.

Make sure that pots cooking have covers on them. This saves time and fuel.

When you boil water, you should remember that wildly churning and turning water is the same temperature as a mild mannered boil. Turn it down.

Baking brownies?

Turn off the heat before they're done. Let the residuals finish the cooking. Don't peek. Each opening of the oven door costs a 20 to 70 degree drop in temperature. Use a clock to time their baking.

TRASH TRAGEDY

Litter is bad.

Smokey the Bear doesn't like it. First Ladies don't like it. Park rangers and the highway patrol don't like it. School teachers and preachers don't like it. Nobody likes litter.

Most of the reasons for not littering sound like the reasons you hear for not wearing your socks two days in a row. It smells bad, it's not respectable.

Here are some better reasons for not littering:

Litter can be dangerous to all sorts of wildlife. Birds get hung up in strings. Animals get strangled by pop tops and plastic wraps. Small animals fall into bottles or cans. If they can't get out they are either fried, frozen, or starved to death.

Garbage tossed out along a highway attracts scavenger animals. Here they are exposed to getting hit by a car.

Litter doesn't stand a very good chance of being recycled. It is real waste.

SEND AWAY:

DEADLY THROWAWAYS

If you need more convincing, send for a booklet called "Deadly Throwaways." It has some really sad pictures of animals who have been littered to death. It should send you scurrying to pick up not only your trash but any you encounter. It says the best way to fight litter is to make less of it. It has some ideas for making things a "litter" better.

Write to:

Defenders of Wildlife
1244 Nineteenth Street
Washington, D. C.
20036

THE NO-BAG GAME

One easy thing to do is to start *not* collecting paper bags. This seems like an easy thing to do, but it isn't.

People who work in stores desperately want to give you a bag. Before you can blink your eye, your two pieces of bubble gum are wrapped up in an ocean of brown paper that you didn't want and certainly don't need.

So next time be quick and outwit the bagger. Smile and say in a friendly but firm way, "No thanks, I don't need a bag." (If you are in the mood you might say something like, "Spend a bag — spoil a forest.") Then take your purchase and shove it into your pocket or backpack. This book has directions for simple packs you can make.

Don't forget to take the tag so the store detective doesn't mistake your noble no-bag exterior for that of a shoplifter. You might even keep a bagging average. Divide the trips to the store by the times you escaped without getting a bag.

WRAPPING IT UP

America has a whole industry that is dedicated to wrapping up things. There are masterminds who see how many pieces of plastic and paper they can wrap around even the simplest of objects. One has to admire the cunning methods they have for mummifying a stick of gum or housing a hamburger for those long seconds they linger on the fast food counter. After awhile you begin to believe you need your bread with a plastic skin around it. Well, you don't. In France people buy their bread with no wrapping. You are likely to see naked loaves sticking out of their brief cases, baby buggies, or under their arms. In Mexico you might see an Indian lady with a couple of pounds of lemons, a melon, and her youngest kid wrapped up in a shawl. In England fish and chips are served on yesterday's newspaper.

People have been getting along for a long time without wasting their resources on shrink wrap and styrofoam. You can start by developing some wrapping consciousness. Try not to buy over-packaged stuff. Don't take the bags. Let manufacturers know what you think of their packages by writing them nasty notes on their shrink wrap.

WHAT TO DO
WITH AN OLD BAG

America is the land of plenty, at least when it comes to brown bags. Every house has a cupboard jammed with all sorts of bags. Even the most militant nonbag takers have a way of col-

lecting more bags than they can line the garbage can with. Here are some ways to have some fun using bags.

BIG COSTUMES FOR SHORT KIDS.

CUT ARM HOLES

MASKS FOR BIG KIDS.

BAG EFFIGIES STUFF THEM WITH PAPER. GLUE ON BITS AND PIECES. ATTACH THEM TO A STANDING OR CARRYING STICK.

BAG BOMBS

FILL WITH AIR.

BAG BUILDING BLOCKS; STUFF SHOPPING BAGS WITH NEWSPAPER. STAPLE THEM SHUT. BUILD.

FOLD UP BOX

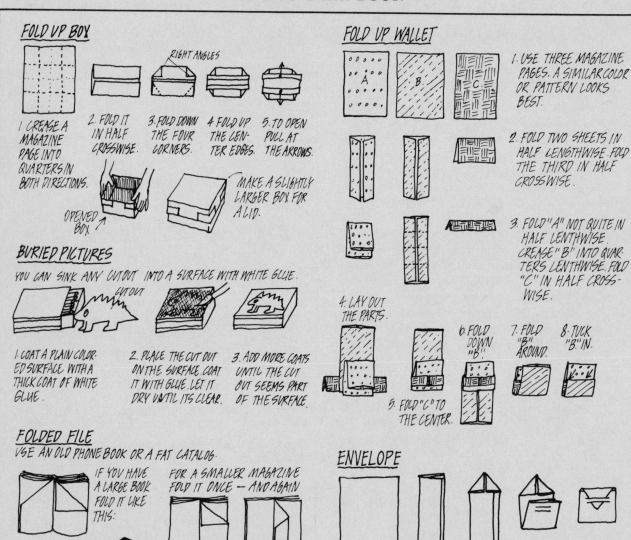

RIGHT ANGLES

1. CREASE A MAGAZINE PAGE INTO QUARTERS IN BOTH DIRECTIONS.

2. FOLD IT IN HALF CROSSWISE.

3. FOLD DOWN THE FOUR CORNERS.

4. FOLD UP THE CENTER EDGES.

5. TO OPEN PULL AT THE ARROWS.

OPENED BOX

MAKE A SLIGHTLY LARGER BOX FOR A LID.

BURIED PICTURES

YOU CAN SINK ANY CUT OUT INTO A SURFACE WITH WHITE GLUE.

CUT OUT

1. COAT A PLAIN COLORED SURFACE WITH A THICK COAT OF WHITE GLUE.

2. PLACE THE CUT OUT ON THE SURFACE. COAT IT WITH GLUE. LET IT DRY UNTIL ITS CLEAR.

3. ADD MORE COATS UNTIL THE CUT OUT SEEMS PART OF THE SURFACE.

FOLDED FILE

USE AN OLD PHONE BOOK OR A FAT CATALOG.

IF YOU HAVE A LARGE BOOK FOLD IT LIKE THIS:

FOR A SMALLER MAGAZINE FOLD IT ONCE — AND AGAIN

STAPLE THE COVERS TOGETHER FOR A CIRCULAR FILE

A SMALL MAGAZINE MAKES A HALF FILE.

FOLD UP WALLET

A   B   C

1. USE THREE MAGAZINE PAGES. A SIMILAR COLOR OR PATTERN LOOKS BEST.

2. FOLD TWO SHEETS IN HALF LENGTHWISE. FOLD THE THIRD IN HALF CROSSWISE.

3. FOLD "A" NOT QUITE IN HALF LENTHWISE. CREASE "B" INTO QUARTERS LENTHWISE. FOLD "C" IN HALF CROSSWISE.

4. LAY OUT THE PARTS.

5. FOLD "C" TO THE CENTER.

6. FOLD DOWN "B"

7. FOLD "B" AROUND.

8. TUCK "B" IN.

ENVELOPE

1. START WITH A MAGAZINE PAGE.

2. FOLD IT INTO THIRDS.

3. FOLD ONE END TO A POINT.

4. FOLD THE BOTTOM TO THE TOP. CUT A SLIT AND THREAD THE POINT THROUGH.

PRESTO CHANGO PAPER

There is more than one way to recycle magazines. You can trade them with a friend. Or you can bundle them up and take them to the Goodwill or a local hospital that needs some reading material.

Another way is to look at those old magazines as raw material. Lurking among those pages are all sorts of nifty items like wallets, puzzles, beads, boxes, and holders. Some of these are simple folded things. Some need scissors and glue. All are pretty simple. Get ready for some things to do with your tired old magazines.

JUNK BUSINESS

You can make some money and help out the earth at the same time by going into the recycling business. You don't have to collect tons of paper and pounds of smashed glass. Start small. Specialize. Like they say, "Every litter bit helps."

CANS INTO CASH

You can get 15 cents a pound for all-aluminum cans. If somebody around your house drinks a lot of beer, you're in luck. Just 23 cans and you've earned yourself 15 cents. Let your neighbors know you are interested in their cans.

Prospect for cans. You will find them anywhere people have been: campsites, beaches, under bleachers after a day at the races. Serious can prospectors will take a gunny sack along on vacation. America's roadsides are rich with deposits. Smash them flat so they don't crowd you out of the back seat. You might carry along a magnet to make sure you don't have any worthless imposters. (A magnet won't stick to any part of an aluminum can.) You might be so successful that your mom and dad will say either you or the cans have to go. Never fear. There are collection centers all over America. Check in the local phone book. Or write away for a directory before you go.

FOILED

During the war aluminum was scarce. Kids did their bit by collecting tinfoil balls. Kids went to great lengths to build the biggest balls on the block.

You can start a foil ball today. The aluminum recycling center will buy it from you as long as it's been cleaned. How much do you think a basketball sized one might be worth?

SEND AWAY:
CAN CENTERS

Write for your directory of aluminum recycling centers. It's free from:

Reynolds Aluminum Recycling Company
P. O. Box 27003
Richmond, Virginia
23261

SEND AWAY:
RECYCLING
IN A BIG WAY

If you have a lot of energy and some space, you might consider starting a neighborhood recycling center. Be warned, you won't make much money and it's hard messy work.

Still interested? Send 50 cents for a booklet called, "How to Start a Neighborhood Recycling Center." Send it to:

Ecology Center
2179 Allston Way
Berkeley, California
94704

LIVER LIDS

Liver lids are those plastic tops that you get from meat market containers that hold things like liver and brains. They have a red rim around the outside and are clear on the inside. If your mom buys liver, you're in luck. Collect all you can, get out your felt markers, turn the oven on to 400 degrees and get ready to have some fun.

Liver lids have the magical ability to shrink down into a disc, so anything you draw on a lid shrinks too, looking a little like stained glass. You can hang the results in windows or wear them round your neck or use them for a key chain.

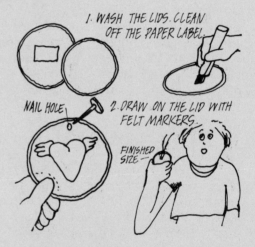

Here's what to do:
1. Wash the lids.
2. Clean off the paper labels.
3. Draw on the lid. Experiment with markers. Some stick better than others.
4. If you want to hang it, punch a hole into the clear part *before* it goes into the oven.
5. Put the lid on a cookie sheet and put it in the oven for about two minutes.

Amazing isn't it? Quick, press it flat with a pancake turner before it cools. If it won't lie flat, heat it, and press it again.

SEND AWAY:
OLD TIRES MAKE NIFTY NESTS

There is a free information sheet on how to make old tires into homes for doves, wood ducks, woodpeckers and squirrels. You might need some strong-arm help cutting and shaping tough old tires. If you have that, you need some ideas. Write for "Wildlife Homes from Old Tires, OSAn17, 2702. It is free from:

Publications
University of California
Division of Agricultural Sciences
1422 South 10th Street
Richmond, California
94804

HOW TO WEAR TIN CAN TAPS: STOMP

BEER CAN TAP SHOES

Feel like a little shuffle-off-to-Buffalo? Make some instant tap shoes with a pair of aluminum cans. Don't forget to recycle them when the show is over.

Fit your can shoes over your regular shoes by stomping squarely on the middle of the cans. A little music. . . and you're in business.

PLASTIC BOTTLE BRACELET

Plastic bottles present a special challenge. They can't be recycled like paper, bottles, or cans. In order to recycle plastic, you have to think up a new use for it. You can turn bottles into bracelets. All it takes is scissors.

CUT SLICES FROM A PLASTIC BOTTLE. TRY THEM TO CHECK THE FIT.

PAINT THEM WITH ACRYLICS. TRY CUTTING SOME FANCY SHAPES.

TIN BADGES

Some cans have beautiful, painted on labels, especially ones housing fancy foreign foods. If you have strong hands and a good pair of tin snips, you can wear these bits of tin can art.

1. Cut out the part you want. Be careful, steel edges can give you some savage cuts.

2. Sand or file the edges smooth.

3. Tape on a safety pin fastener or buy a proper pin back at the dime store. Stick it on with household cement.

RUBBER BAND BALL

When the Spanish adventurers came to the New World they were amazed to see the Indians playing a game with a ball made of a material that acted in a most mysterious way. When the ball hit something hard it would leap away from whatever it struck. The Indians had discovered that a sap from a certain sort of tree had elastic properties. They were the first to make rubber balls.

Since then people have figured out a million ways to use this stretchy sap. One way is the good old rubber band. You can get some good bounces out of a handful of rubber bands, if you know how to roll them. Here's how.

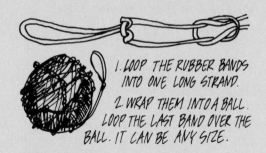

1. LOOP THE RUBBER BANDS INTO ONE LONG STRAND.

2. WRAP THEM INTO A BALL. LOOP THE LAST BAND OVER THE BALL. IT CAN BE ANY SIZE.

BUSINESS ON TWO WHEELS

Did you know that riding a bike is 28 times more efficient than riding in a car?

Walking is 17 times as efficient.

Buses are 4 times as efficient.

Trains are 2.5 times as efficient.

Only flying a plane uses more energy.

With those figures in mind, how 'bout saving some fossil fuel and making yourself a little money at the same time? You can do both by starting your own errand-delivery service.

Let the people on your block know about your service. Old folks especially would be interested in somebody who is willing to do some footwork around town. You might even put a few posters up on your street and at the local supermarket. Give out cards to prospective customers with your phone number and when you're able to work.

Decide how much to charge. Something like 25 cents a trip each way. Or you could charge 50 cents for every half hour.

P. S. Getting a business started may take a little time. But once people find out how handy and dependable you are, you should have some steady customers.

13
GAMES

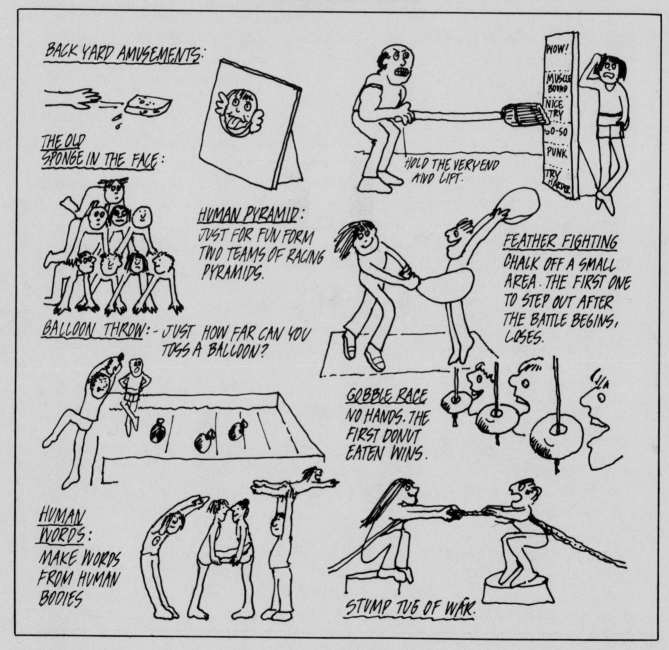

BACK YARD AMUSEMENTS:

THE OLD SPONGE IN THE FACE:

HOLD THE VERY END AND LIFT.

WOW! MUSCLE BOUND NICE TRY SO-SO PUNK TRY HARDER

HUMAN PYRAMID: JUST FOR FUN FORM TWO TEAMS OF RACING PYRAMIDS.

FEATHER FIGHTING CHALK OFF A SMALL AREA. THE FIRST ONE TO STEP OUT AFTER THE BATTLE BEGINS, LOSES.

BALLOON THROW: - JUST HOW FAR CAN YOU TOSS A BALLOON?

GOBBLE RACE NO HANDS. THE FIRST DONUT EATEN WINS.

HUMAN WORDS: MAKE WORDS FROM HUMAN BODIES

STUMP TUG OF WAR.

VACANT LOT AMUSEMENT PARK

A backyard carnival or vacant lot amusement park can be a good time for a lot of people. It's a good way to make your next birthday party really special or it can be a fun way to raise money for a worthy cause like a Save-the-Whales organization.

First you should decide how many people you want at your event. Then pick a site. If you are expecting only a few, just a corner of the backyard will do. If there will be many people you might look around for a vacant lot to borrow. In any case, check to make sure nobody will arrest you for trespassing.

Second, decide if this is a free-for-all-just-for-fun event or if you will charge money. You can charge one price for admission or you can sell tickets for each event. Keep your prices low.

Next you need to invite people to your amusement park. Give out handbills or put up posters telling about your event: when, where, and how much it costs.

All that is left now is to build your amusements. Here are some ideas.

HARE AND HOUNDS

This is a good breathtaking chase game for a bunch of kids. It is best played in a wide area with lots of places to hide. You might want to limit the playing space by drawing up some boundaries. Choose a team of kids to be the hares. The rest are hounds.

To play:

1. Hares get a roll of toilet paper and a two minute head start.

2. They lay a trail by securing pieces of paper to trees, under rocks, etc. Each paper should be within seeing distance of the last. Trickiness is allowed.

3. Hounds track hares by collecting paper clues. The object is for the hares to make it back to the starting place without being seen.

Don't forget to gather up all the paper clues before starting the next game.

ANOTHER WAY TO PLAY

1. Hares get about 30 slices of potato, 50 beans, and a ten-minute start

2. The trail should have a potato about every twenty yards. Plant beans about every five yards.

3. The object of this game is not to sight the hares, but to collect as many clues as you can. Score 1 point for every potato slice and 5 points for every bean collected.

Lay the crookedest, most diabolical trail you can. Count on your rivals to do the same. Don't worry about the lost pieces. The local wildlife will put them on their dinner menus.

ARROW

A sidewalk version of Hare and Hounds. This time the trail team carries a piece of chalk. They leave a trail of arrows chalked on sidewalks, fences, car tires, rocks, whatever is handy. They

are chased and sighted. Confusion can be avoided if each round is played with a different color of chalk.

CAPTURE THE FLAG

This is a great old classic to play all day in the wide open spaces. Of course it can be fun in a shorter version than this one too.

Get ready:

1. Divide into two teams.
2. Mark the bounds. Divide the area in half. Territory should include trees, bushes, and

ups and downs. If you are playing at camp, you just might want to divide it right down the middle.

3. Each team has a flag, which is put at the far end of the territory. It should be guarded. Mark off a square to be the jail.

To play:

The object of this game is to capture the other team's flag and carry it to your own territory.

1. The game starts with each team around its flag. Commandos and border patrols, a jailer and guards are chosen, and raids are planned to bring back the flag.

2. A commando is caught by putting arms around him long enough to say "caught, caught, caught." The commando then is escorted to jail deep inside your territory.

3. Jailbirds can be freed by being touched by a free commando of their team. You can free a whole group of jailbirds at once if they've joined hands.

This game goes on until it's lunch time or until it rains or until somebody captures the flag.

BIKE RODEO

This is a fun thing to do with a bunch of other kids on bikes. It could be part of a vacant lot amusement park or you could stage a bike rodeo for the kids in your scout troop or the kids on your block. You should have some prizes and a referee. Rodeos are best on a big flat blacktop area like a school playground, but dirt will do.

Here are some ideas for the events. Of course, there is no rule that says you can't set up a practice course in your driveway.

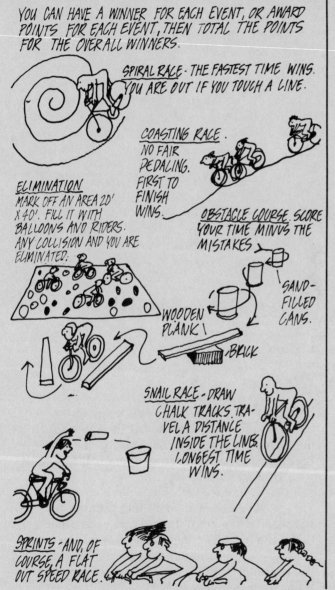

YOU CAN HAVE A WINNER FOR EACH EVENT, OR AWARD POINTS FOR EACH EVENT, THEN TOTAL THE POINTS FOR THE OVERALL WINNERS.

SPIRAL RACE · THE FASTEST TIME WINS. YOU ARE OUT IF YOU TOUCH A LINE.

COASTING RACE · NO FAIR PEDALING. FIRST TO FINISH WINS.

ELIMINATION MARK OFF AN AREA 20' X 40'. FILL IT WITH BALLOONS AND RIDERS. ANY COLLISION AND YOU ARE ELIMINATED.

OBSTACLE COURSE. SCORE YOUR TIME MINUS THE MISTAKES

SAND-FILLED CANS.

WOODEN PLANK

BRICK

SNAIL RACE - DRAW CHALK TRACKS. TRAVEL A DISTANCE INSIDE THE LINES. LONGEST TIME WINS.

SPRINTS - AND, OF COURSE, A FLAT OUT SPEED RACE.

KICK THE CAN

This game was collected right off the street from a bunch of kids who were having a good time playing it.

All you need is a can.

To play:

1. Drop the can on the ground. It's best on some hard surface that clatters. Choose someone to be "it."

2. "It" stands near the can and closes his eyes counting to 100. Everybody scatters and hides.

3. "It" then tries to find and tag the kids hiding before they are able to sneak up and kick the can. The first person tagged is "it" for the next game.

Variation: The rules can be switched so that tagged people are in jail. They can be set free by being touched by another untagged person. This game isn't over till everybody is in jail.

POM POM POMAWAY

This game is also called British Bulldog. It is best played with a mob of kids.

Get ready:

Draw up a boundary, a big rectangle long enough to get a good run in. One or two persons are "it." They stand in the middle of the field. Everybody else line up at one end.

To play:

1. "It" gives a signal by shouting "Pom Pom Pomaway."

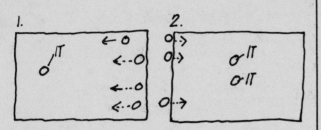

2. Kids on the ends run across the field, trying to avoid capture. They are captured if an "it" grabs them long enough to say "Pom Pom Pomaway."

3. Captured kids join the "its."

4. The winner is the last person to be captured.

FLY

Fly is a good game for a bunch of kids with nimble feet. Clods seldom win at Fly, unless everyone else is having an attack of the clumsies.

To play Fly you will need a level spot and about a dozen thick sticks at least two feet long. The sticks should be an inch or more in diameter so that you have something to step over.

To play:

1. Set the sticks in railroad-tie fashion about a foot apart. Some should be a bit more, some a bit less.

2. Every one lines up and takes a turn going over the obstacle course. You have to step in each space, and you have to go over each stick on one foot. Once you're safely in a space you can touch down with your other foot.

3. You are out if you move a stick even a teeny bit.

4. On the next round, the leader kid gets to pick up the front stick and move it to the rear. The kid can put it impossibly close or inhumanly far. The trick is to move it so you can make it, but nobody else can.

5. The last person left is the winner.

LEG RACING

You need a whole mob of kids for this one, the more the better. When everybody finds a partner you should have one person left over to be the caller.

Getting set: Get the partners to form two lines facing each other. Then they sit down with their legs together, the soles of their feet touching their partners' feet. Each pair gets a number from one to however many pairs there are.

How to play:

1. The caller yells out a random number.

2. When the pair with that number gets the signal, they jump up and race each other down the leg maze, then circle around the outside and go over the remaining legs. The first of the pair back to their place wins and scores a point for their side.

LEAVE ENOUGH
SPACE TO STEP
THROUGH.

3. You're out if you don't step in every space between the pairs of legs or if you run the wrong way.

This game is over when every pair has had a turn. This one is so exciting that everybody will probably want at least another round.

SEND AWAY:

GAMES MAG

Here is a sample page from Games "Mag," a nifty little publication that describes itself as a "magazine for teachers, students, parents, and anyone else who likes games. Not only are there math games, but also action games, word games, non-western games, magic, illusions and puzzles." It costs $6.00 for nine issues, or you can get a sample copy for 50 cents. Write:

Games Mag
The Center for Open Learning and Teaching
P. O. Box 9434
Berkeley, California
94709

FEATHER THROWING CONTESTS

Native Americans throughout the Southwest and Northwest made darts out of feathers they found or plucked out of birds. They used these feather darts for a number of different games and contests which can easily be played at home or school.

Bone Dart

Corncob Dart

First find some feathers. To make them into throwable darts wrap some strips of lead, of the sort used as sinkers for fishing lines, around the tip of the feather. Then wrap leather or some yarn around the lead and you have a dart.

SINKER

yarn

One common game was played with feather darts and a hoop made of a bent twig tied at the end. The game consisted of throwing the arrow through the hoop. Each player gets 5 to 10 chances and the one who gets the dart through the hoop the most times wins.

More elaborate targets can easily be made.

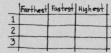

3 hoops hanging from a branch.

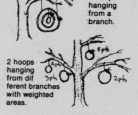

2 hoops hanging from different branches with weighted areas.

5 pts
4 pts
3 pts
2 pts

It is also possible to have dart throwing contests. The contests can be for seeing who can:
1) throw the dart the farthest;
2) throw their dart the highest;
3) keep their dart in the air for the longest time;
4) throw their dart the fastest.

	Farthest	Fastest	Highest
1			
2			
3			

To measure who throws their dart the highest the dart can be attached to a ball of light string — a stop watch would help with timing in the speed and duration contests — the results could be made into a chart.

It would be interesting to discover whether different kinds of feathers are best suited to these different contests or whether there is a best overall feather.

4

JACK STRAWS

This game also goes by the name of Spillikins and Pick Up Sticks. You need to find about 30 thin straight sticks. Paint them in colors, check the scoring chart.

Toss the sticks with the black one in the center. Pick them up one by one, being careful not to move anything else. If you do, you are out. Your opponent gets a chance to outscore you.

Score chart:

1 black	=	10 points
7 greens	=	8 points
7 blues	=	6 points
7 yellows	=	4 points
7 reds	=	2 points

POMMAWONGA

Get your jollies from junk. Coming up are a number of games you can make from throwaways. Pommawonga is one.

This game has many names. It goes by Toss and Catch, Ring and Pin, Hoop and Pole, to name a few. Indians in the Americas called it Zimba, Gazinth, and Pommawonga. It was made many ways from whatever was handy: wood, bone, or ivory. Read on to find out how to make your own game of Pommawonga.

1. Ask the butcher what he has in the way of soup bones. Pick out one that is tube shaped.

2. Ask him to cut it into 3/8 inch slices. You should have about five slices.

3. Take your bones home and clean them. You can bury them and let the organisms in the soil clean them. If you don't want to wait for a few weeks, boil them in some detergent water.

4. Assemble them as shown.

To play:

Toss the bones and see how many you can catch on a toss. Some people had the habit of gambling on their tosses.

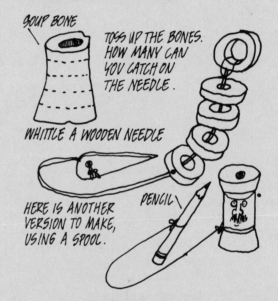

SOUP BONE

TOSS UP THE BONES. HOW MANY CAN YOU CATCH ON THE NEEDLE.

WHITTLE A WOODEN NEEDLE

HERE IS ANOTHER VERSION TO MAKE, USING A SPOOL.

PENCIL

KILLER

This is another game that needs a lot of kids but no equipment. You need to choose a killer so that his identity remains a secret. A good way to do this is to pass out folded sheets of paper to everyone. One is marked for the killer.

To play, each person sits so they can see everyone's face. The object is to discover who is the killer before he gets you. The killer kills with a wink. If you are winked at, you have to fall down dead.

Eye contact must be constant. You can't close your eyes to the killer.

YO-YO

In the Phillipines it was used as a weapon. An attacker would hide in a tree and bonk an enemy on the head with it, often leaving the victim quite dead.

The yo-yo was popular with Egyptians. It was not known in Europe until about 1790 when a French yo-yo craze was started by monks returning from China. Yo-yo fever struck America in 1920 when Mr. Duncan coined the name we now use.

BUTTON YO-YO

You need two big matching coat buttons, some cord, and a bit of wire to make your own yo-yo. Here's how:

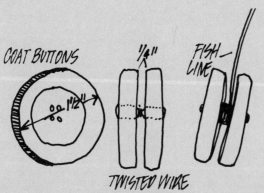

COAT BUTTONS — 1/4" — FISH LINE — TWISTED WIRE

ESKIMO YO-YO

The native people of Alaska call this game "Innuit." You can make a version of it with some string and two wooden spools or a pair of rubber balls.

To make the yo-yo:

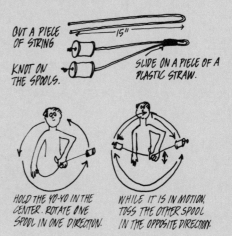

CUT A PIECE OF STRING 15" — KNOT ON THE SPOOLS. — SLIDE ON A PIECE OF A PLASTIC STRAW.

HOLD THE YO-YO IN THE CENTER. ROTATE ONE SPOOL IN ONE DIRECTION. — WHILE IT IS IN MOTION, TOSS THE OTHER SPOOL IN THE OPPOSITE DIRECTION.

CHIVAS

This is a skill game from Mexico. All you need is a handful of beans and a hole big enough to hold your beans.

To play:

1. Divide the beans so that every player gets an equal number. Ten is a good amount.

2. Taking turns, each player tosses his beans into the hole. He then collects the ones that land in the hole.

3. One at a time these survivor beans are placed on the back of the hands, tossed into the air, and caught in the palm.

The person who catches the most wins.

14

TRIPS

GOING SOMEWHERE?

Summer is vacation time. For a lot of kids vacation means taking a trip. Whether you go on a picnic to the lake, ride the bus to Grandma's house, backpack for a week in the mountains, or ride across America with your whole family and the dog, getting there is half the fun.

You can learn a lot on a trip just talking to people, tasting new food, and exploring new towns. Even when you find yourself lost in a new place, you can learn about yourself. Take a look out the window, you'll see things you never saw before.

BACK SEAT NAVIGATOR

A lot of families take trips in the summer. After the first exciting hour in the back seat of the car, things can get pretty dull. You can only ask, "How much longer before we get there?" a couple of times before the tone of the driver's voice tells you its going to be risky to ask one more time.

Learn how to read the road map and you won't have to ask. In fact, if you become an ace map reader, you'll be asked if there's a rest stop up ahead or how many miles it is to the next town. If you've got the map and the answer to the questions, that makes you the navigator. As navigator you'll have a bigger say in what direction your trip takes.

Besides it will make life in the back seat or any seat a bit more exciting.

WHERE TO GET YOUR MAPS

Maps can be found in lots of places. Of course, map makers make them for a whole lot of reasons. And they have all sorts of different information on them.

If your parents belong to the Automobile Association of America, you can get all sorts of free maps there. They have big state maps and more detailed maps of counties.

Gas stations have good road maps with lots of details. You will have to buy these, but they don't cost a lot. You might shop around and hold out for the more colorful ones. They are easier to read. Gas stations should have both city street maps and highway maps.

You local Chamber of Commerce might have a free map of your town; or if you live in a bigger town, you can try the Tourist Bureau.

State Highway Departments will often supply you with free maps. Write to Department of Highways in the capital city of the state you're interested in.

So far we've been talking about road maps, which leaves a lot of country in between. National and state parks supply maps of many of these areas.

SEND AWAY:

GUIDE TO LITTLE-KNOWN WONDERS

If your family is planning a summer trip, you might work in some little-known national and natural wonders. Ever hear of Boll Weevil Monument in Coffee County, Alabama? Or Dinosaur State Park (site of 1,000 plus dinosaur prints) near Hartford, Connecticut? Or the last of the tall grass prairie, Flint Hills, Kansas? All these and 73 more interesting spots are listed in a booklet called, "76 Places to Visit," the conservationist's guide to historic landmarks.

You can get one copy free from:

National Wildlife Federation
1412 Sixteenth Street, N. W.
Washington, D. C.
20036

Additional copies are 35 cents.

TRIP JOURNAL

Keeping a notebook of your travels can be a fun thing to do. Later on, it can be even more fun to dig out of your stash of forgotten treasures and look over. You'll find all those bits and pieces will have a way of making your memory bank cough up the long forgotten.

Before you start on your trip, make or buy a notebook (there are instructions for making your own journal in this book). You won't need anything too large. Choose a size you like. If you plan to do a lot of drawings, plain paper looks better than lined. Get a pen or pencils you like to write with or watercolors.

Remember to bring a sharpener if you use pencils.

Your journal can have anything you want in it. Since it is a trip journal, don't forget to put in where you've gone and when. You might even paste in sections of the map. Add in bits you find along the way like matchbook covers

or funky placemats or coasters or leaflets from museums or parks. Paste in postcards of your favorite spots. Add drawings of things you don't want to forget like funny happenings or conversations.

You can even start drawing collections of things like mountains or weather vanes. Or funny signs. Or rubbings. Or drawings of outlandish mail boxes.

MAKING A JOURNAL

Making a book is fun. If you are making one to take along on your vacation, plan to do it before you go. Bookmaking is not something you can do in the back seat of a car.

You will need some cardboard, some cloth tape (from the hardware store), some heavy thread, and some fancy paper or cloth for the cover. And you need paper for the pages; you can use shelf paper, bag paper, or drawing paper — whatever you like.

Here is what to do:

SIMPLE SOFT-COVER JOURNAL

1. YOU WILL NEED 8 PAGES OF TYPING PAPER + 1 PAGE OF HEAVY PAPER FOR THE COVER.

2. FOLD THE PAGES IN HALF SEPARATELY. STAPLE THEM TOGETHER ALONG THE FOLD.

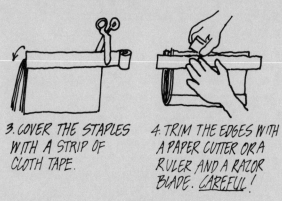

3. COVER THE STAPLES WITH A STRIP OF CLOTH TAPE.

4. TRIM THE EDGES WITH A PAPER CUTTER OR A RULER AND A RAZOR BLADE. <u>CAREFUL</u>!

SPY

You can make your own card game to take along on your next trip. Each player gets a number of cards, each with a picture of a thing you might see out the window along the way. When players see any of the things pictured on their cards, they say, "Spy" (so everybody else can make sure they are playing fair). Then they discard. The first one to spot everything and discard all of his or her cards, wins.

FOR MORE PERMANENT CARDS, COVER THE PICTURES WITH PLASTIC FILM. YOU CAN BUY IT BY THE HALF YARD AT DIME STORES. ASK FOR CLEAR CONTACT PAPER.

1. CUT THE CONTACT PAPER TO SIZE.

2. PEEL AWAY THE BACKING.

3. PRESS IT ON, AND TRIM.

You can make your own deck with a package of three by five inch cards. Make about two dozen to begin with. Each card needs a word or a picture of a likely object on one side. You can draw them or cut out magazine pictures and glue them on.

Here are some ideas for "Spy" objects: stray hub cap, the fuzz, railroad crossing, a hawk, dust devil, crop duster, flock of birds, school, American flag, lone tree, windmill, something on three legs, car built before 1960, a mammal, a car filled to capacity, tent, mud, bathtub, bridge, horn honk, somebody who waves, bike path, baby animal.

SEASICK IN THE CAR

You might wonder how you can be seasick in the car. That's easy. You are not really sick from the sea. In the same way that you get sick from the motions of oceans, you can get sick from the motions of planes or cars.

What happens is that your balance gets upset. Deep inside your ears you have devices called the semicircular canals. These canals are filled with fluid and are lined with special hairs which sense movement when your body changes position. In short, your canals let you know what's up and what's down, and riding motion can make them pretty confused. It happens like this.

Usually the fluid sits quietly in the bottom of your canals. Quick or violent motions send the fluid sloshing into motion. You feel dizzy and unbalanced. The rocking motions of a car or boat also set the fluid into motion, causing that awful feeling in your stomach.

You will be glad to know that eventually your body can adjust to these rocking motions. However don't expect one trip in the back seat through the mountains to cure you for life. Read on for some hints on what to do until the road straightens out.

IF YOU FEEL SICK

Do not try to forget how sick you feel by reading. Reading in a moving car makes even the steadiest person queasy.

Try lying down flat. This position can fool your semicircular canals into thinking you are standing up and walking. Rocking motions are a lot like walking motions, at least to your inner ears.

Move to the front seat. There is less motion up front.

Perhaps your parents can get you an anti-motion sickness pill which is available from any drug store.

If you think you might be sick, get yourself some airsickness bags like they do on the airlines. Make sure you get the window seat. (This trick works every time for reserving a window space.)

TRIP KIT

There is nothing worse than suddenly getting the urge to play Tic-Tac-Toe and discovering that you remembered the paper, but forgot the pencils. You can solve that problem forever with a trip kit.

Trip kits are a box full of tools and things that you think you will need on your journey. Later on it will also be stuff that you have collected along the way. After you know where you are going, you can decide on what you will need. Don't forget some gum and a good book for emergencies. A shoe box should be about the right size for a trip kit. Now all you have to do is remember the box.

YOU MIGHT BRING: BINOCULARS, A COMPASS, A GOOD BOOK, POCKET-KNIFE, MAGNIFYING GLASS, A JOURNAL, PENCILS, SPY CARDS.

DON'T FORGET SOME TREATS LIKE GUM.

TRIP KIT

BUG JAR

COLLECT FAST FOOD BOXES FOR SPECIMENS.

COLORED EARTH COLLECTION

In Victorian times people liked to bring home bottles of colored earths as souvenirs of their journey. Some rare places have soils of many colors in one area. They usually have names like the Painted Desert. Usually you will have to travel around to pick up a change in the earth's colors. Vacation is a perfect time to collect colored earths.

Bring a spoon and some little plastic bags along on your trip. Cliffs and shores are good places to look. Coarse sandy soils look best in bottles. Here's how to display your collection.

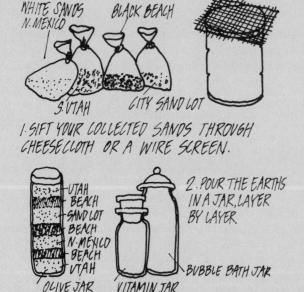

WHITE SANDS N. MEXICO   BLACK BEACH   S. UTAH   CITY SAND LOT

1. SIFT YOUR COLLECTED SANDS THROUGH CHEESECLOTH OR A WIRE SCREEN.

2. POUR THE EARTHS IN A JAR, LAYER BY LAYER.

UTAH BEACH — SAND LOT BEACH — N. MEXICO BEACH — UTAH — OLIVE JAR

VITAMIN JAR   BUBBLE BATH JAR

MIRAGE

Looking ahead on the highway, you sometimes see shimmering patches of water up ahead. You drive and drive and never get your wheels wet. That's because what you saw was not water at all; it was a mirage.

Mirages are tricks that the light plays on your eyes. On a warm day over a paved road there is a hot layer of air. This hot air layer can bend light. Instead of seeing the road, you see light rays from the sky. The hot air layer acts like a prism or mirror. The road ahead shimmers with a silvery glow that you mistake for water.

FATA MORGANA

There are a number of strange mirages that are caused by the atmosphere distorting light rays. One of the rarest and most astounding is called fata morgana. Over the Mediterranean Sea between Italy and Sicily sometimes castles rise out of the sea, ever changing, growing, and collapsing. According to legend these castles are the home of the fairy Morgana.

SEND AWAY:

STATE BIRDS AND BUGS

Do you know the state mammal of Minnesota or the state flower of Florida or the state insect of Indiana? You can find out in the National Wildlife Federation's list called, "Official Birds, Mammals, Trees, Flowers, Insects, and Fish of the United States." You can use this leaflet as the basis of a quiz game. It would be nice to bring along with you on vacation. By the time you get to Grandma's in Kankakee, you should be an expert on official state wildlife. One copy is free from:

Education Servicing
National Wildlife Federation
1412 Sixteenth Street, N. W.
Washington, D. C.
20036

WHAT'S IN A NAME?

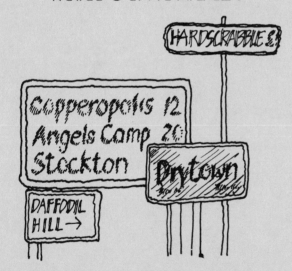

"Deers Ears — 10 Miles"

Sometimes a road sign can wake you right up out of a half sleep and make you really curious about this place, "Deers Ears."

Names on the map can tell you a lot. Dry Lake and Salt Springs are good clues to how a place might look. Santa Fe and Terre Haute tell you something about the people who did the naming, if you know Spanish and French. You can be sure that Jack Ass Hill wasn't named by a schoolmarm and that Harmony Heights wasn't thought up by a rough-and-tumble miner. Names went in and out of fashion. For instance, Georgetown, named in honor of King George of England, was named before the Revolutionary War was fought. And it doesn't take much imagination to figure out that a place called Radio is a fairly new town. Many names have fascinating stories tied up with them: names like Hangtown and Donner Pass.

Be on the lookout for names and the stories they tell.

NAMES FROM THE LAND

Red Bluff, Cedar Rapids, Salt Lake City, Grand Canyon are all places which take their names from the nearby natural features. This is probably the oldest way of naming, and it happens in many languages. Of course, it could be from a breathtaking natural feature like Buffalo, Catfish Alley, or Elkville.

BORROWED NAMES

Early settlers to the new world brought with them the names of their homelands and applied them liberally to the landscape. We have *New* Orleans, *New* Mexico, *New* York, *New* London, *New* Jersey, *New* Haven. Sometimes they didn't bother to add "New," but adopted the name of an already famous place like Amsterdam, Toledo, Cambridge. Adoption was very popular. For instance, towns in 14 different states in the USA are called Cambridge after the original town in England, not to mention Cambridge City, Cambridge Junction, Cambridge Port, Cambridge Springs (a case of Yankee ingenuity sitting around with its feet up). In fact, if you compare our map with a map of the world, you will notice an embarrassing amount of borrowing on our part.

INDIAN NAMES

Native American names didn't begin to appear on the map until after 1850. One reason was that the Indians kept their maps in their heads. Another was that the settlers who did make maps, did their best to remove all traces of Indians from the land.

Indians were "rediscovered" around 1850. Suddenly they were considered to be "noble savages," except for out west where they were still being pushed off their lands. Indian names became romantic.

By this time the old Indian names had been long forgotten. No matter. Any Indian name or something that sounded close to an Indian name would do. Florida Indian names appeared in New England, Plains Indian names showed up in California. Sometimes a word was remodeled to make it more "poetic." Nibthaska was changed to Nebraska. Sometimes the word was saved, but the meaning was lost. Mississippi means "Big River," not "Father of the Waters."

All America has a number of Indian words, like Sekonk, Massachusetts, Yolla Bolly, Walla Walla, and Wichita. Then, of course, there's Chaubunagungamaug Pond.

FOREIGN NAMES

Look across your map and you will see some strange looking words. Yup, foreign. Well, not English. You will notice smatterings of Spanish names in Florida and a rather thick swath of them down the coast of California and into the Southwest. French names lurk in Louisiana and up the Mississippi, as far as Detroit. (Ahem! You did say, "Du Twah," didn't you?) Sharp eyes will pick up scattered bits of German, Dutch, and Welsh.

PEOPLE NAMES, OR THE ONES WHO GOT THERE FIRST

Many places are named after persons, some famous, some once famous, some not really famous but powerful. Mountains have a way of being called after important persons. You know Mt. Whitney, highest point in the continental USA, but do you know Mr. Whitney? — didn't think so. How about Mr. Ranier or Mr. Everest or Mr. Lassen?

Towns often take on the names of people they wish to honor. Like Jamestown after Captain James or Georgetown after King George. Sometimes they're named for a powerful family like the Alexanders of Alexandria. Sometimes a pretty lady or local yokel is cause enough for a name: Jenny Lind is such a town. This

Swedish singing star so enchanted the miners, that they named the camp after her. And there is Annapolis, Susanville, and Sedalia. On the masculine side there is Charleston, Danville, and Williamsburg. How many Presidents' names can you find on the map? Yep, you can even count railroad company presidents.

SALES TALK, OR HIGHFALUTIN NAMES

Sun City, Crystal Cove, Hacienda Heights: you can bet these are developer names. Pleasant sounding with a bit of class. These names are meant to sell lots of houses.

People have been trying to sell property with fancy names for quite a while. English words have already been a favorite with real estate folks. America has more than enough Oakglens, Larchmonts, Hilldales, and a wide assortment of Manors, Parks, Vales, and Estates.

Sometimes townsfolk have done a little cosmetic name changing themselves. Like when the people of Mosquito changed their name to Troutdale. And the citizens of Screamerville decided to become the citizens of Chancellor.

COLLECTING NAMES

If you are on the road this summer and run across a name you really like, write it down in your trip journal or photograph it for a collection of your favorite road signs. Ask around the town with the curious name to see if you can find out its history.

If you didn't have any luck (it's not uncommon for a town to forget how it got its name), you can find out more at the town's library. Tell the librarian what you want to know. You will most likely be handed a dictionary of place names. Use it just like a regular dictionary. While you are at it, you might do a little detective work to find out how your town got its name.

P. S. For a laugh you might take a peek at the names Modesto and Pasadena.

NAME GAME

Suffering suffixes, it's a quiz! That's right, ladies and gentlemen, common everyday name endings attached to towns across America.

But do you know what they mean? Take the quiz and learn a thing or two about name calling.

To play: You get one point for every right definition and another point if you can name a place ending in the word. Write the answers on a sheet of paper. Kids can use a map to help with the towns. Adults should know better.

1.	port	11.	boro	21.	neck
2.	burn	12.	burg	22.	mead
3.	butte	13.	gap	23.	hurst
4.	bury	14.	glen	24.	ton
5.	ham	15.	pass	25.	bridge
6.	hole	16.	springs	26.	ford
7.	rapids	17.	mesa	27.	vale
8.	beck	18.	mouth	28.	gulch
9.	bluff	19.	run	29.	mont
10.	dale	20.	ville	30.	polis

For answers see page 160

ADVENTURING AROUND TOWN

Now that you are an expert in reading maps, get out a map of your own town. Find your house on the map. Now mark off the way you get to school and to the store, to your best friend's house, and any other places you go. You'll find you have definite trails through your town like animals have tracks through a forest. Unless you live in a really small place, you will find spots you hardly ever visit, maybe places you've never been. This summer is the perfect time to explore them.

Gather up a friend, pack a lunch or a snack, and set out to explore. You can go on foot or on the bus. (Figuring out how to get around town on the bus can be a real adventure in itself.) Or you can take your bike. A kid can cover a lot of territory on a bike. Better bring a little change in case you need to call home or in case you meet the ice cream man.

Don't forget to tell your mom or dad where you are going and when you plan to be back. If they object, you could invite them to come along, or better yet, have them meet you there — so you have a ride home.

Happy trails.

COMPASS WALK

Do you think you spend your time walking around in circles? If you live in a city, you spend your time walking around in squares or blocks. This is a highly unusual way to get from place to place. Most animals make tracks from place to place in fairly straight fashion. Even in wild areas people tend to stick to the well worn trails.

You can discover some interesting things by getting off the beaten path. The last time I beelined across a meadow I found the grass was full of tiny grey moths, invisible from the path. I also ran into a dead skunk. I got about as close as I've ever come to one in the wild. There was also a bonus of a whole seed collection which I found when I took off my socks.

There is no telling what you will run into.

The best thing for straight-lining it across the countryside is a compass. Pick a wide open space. Pick a direction and follow it in a straight line as far as you can. If you run into something like a cliff or a clump of poison oak, try to go around it and pick up where you left off.

You might try this in town. See how far you get.

SEND AWAY:

HOW TO TAKE CARE OF A MOUNTAIN

Every year more people take to the woods and find they like it outdoors. If you start multiplying the impact of those boots and add in the campsites, fire rings, and garbage that go along with all those folks, the effects can be pretty hard on the land, especially in the fragile places like the high mountains and the deserts. The Sierra Club has a nifty little folder called "The Care and Enjoyment of the Mountains." It has some trail and camp lore plus some very important information about how to enjoy the wilderness without tromping it to death. Everybody should read it. Send a stamped self-addressed envelope to:

Sierra Club
530 Bush St
San Francisco, California
94108

NAME GAME (ANSWERS)

This is a hard quiz even for adults. A good score is more than twenty-five. You are a real whiz if you got more than thirty-five. You probably read maps like most people read books if you got a score of over forty-five.

1. port (Newport) Harbor.
2. burn (Auburn) Scottish for small stream.
3. butte (Butte) French for lone hill with steep sides.
4. bury (Salisbury) English word, cousin of burg.
5. ham (Birmingham) Old English for place of settlement.
6. hole (Woodshole) American trapper lingo for secluded valley.
7. rapids (Grand Rapids) Swift river with white water.
8. beck (Rhinebeck) English for a brook.
9. bluff (Pine Bluff) A high, steep bank.
10. dale (Carbondale) Valley. English.
11. boro (Greensboro) American spelling of Borough. English for a town with special privileges.
12. burg (Gettysburg) Old English for a fortified town.
13. gap (Cumberland Gap) American. A mountain pass where the other side can be seen.
14. glen (Watkins Glen) A secluded narrow valley. English.
15. pass (Grants Pass) A way through the mountains usually around several ridges.
16. springs (Palm Springs) A place where ground water seeps to the surface.
17. mesa (Costa Mesa) A flat-topped hill with steep sides. Also the Spanish word for table.
18. mouth (Portsmouth) Spot where a river empties into the sea.
19. run (Bull Run) Creek. Used in the eastern USA.
20. ville (Nashville) A French word for town.
21. neck (Teaneck) A narrow stretch of land.
22. mead (Sunny Mead) Old English word for meadow.
23. hurst (Pinehurst) Old English word for thicket.
24. ton (Washington) Shortened form of town.
25. bridge (Cambridge) Everybody knows what a bridge is.
26. ford (Hartford) A river crossing, usually a place where a river is shallow.
27. vale (Sunnyvale) Old English for valley.
28. gulch (French Gulch) Dry creek bed. This is a word of the Old West.
29. mont (Belmont) Mountain. French word.
30. polis (Minneapolis) Greek for city.